Also by Douglas E. Schoen

Enoch Powell and the Powellites

Pat: A Biography of Daniel Patrick Moynihan

On the Campaign Trail: The Long Road of Presidential Politics, 1860–2004

The Power of the Vote: Electing Presidents, Overthrowing Dictators, and Promoting Democracy Around the World

Declaring Independence: The Beginning of the End of the Two-Party System

The Threat Closer to Home: Hugo Chavez and the War Against America (with Michael Rowan)

What Makes You Tick? How Successful People Do It—and What You Can Learn from Them (with Michael J. Berland)

The Political Fix: Changing the Game of American Democracy, from the Grass Roots to the White House

Mad as Hell: How the Tea Party Movement Is Fundamentally Remaking Our Two-Party System (with Scott Rasmussen)

Hopelessly Divided: The New Crisis in American Politics and What It Means for 2012 and Beyond

AMERICAN CASINO

The Rigged Game That's Killing Democracy

DOUGLAS E. SCHOEN

Velocity Press

NEW YORK NY

Velocity Press

Designed by: John W Taylor

Library of Congress Cataloging in Publication data is pending.

18 17 16 15 14 13 12   1 2 3 4 5

Contents

To my mother, Carol B. Schoen, whose concern for social justice and equity informed this book—and indeed all that I have ever written.

Note on Campaign Finance Data

As the notes make clear, most of my campaign finance numbers come from two of the most respected nonpartisan organizations conducting research on campaign spending: Open Secrets and the Campaign Finance Institute. At other points I've cited news stories as sources, many of which themselves cite back to these two groups.

Both Open Secrets and CFI have earned widespread commendation from officials across the ideological spectrum, and neither has, to my knowledge, ever had its work questioned. I have used one or the other source somewhat interchangeably in these chapters essentially for convenience: for various data points, one or the other organization might have had the numbers in more accessible form. Their figures do not always agree dollar for dollar—which, I've concluded, says more about the often murky world of campaign finance than it does about their methodologies.

As my primary objective in writing this book was to make an argument about the corrosiveness of money in our politics, not parse exact spending data, I have made no attempt to reconcile one group's numbers with the other's.

Introduction

THE END OF AMERICAN DEMOCRACY?

L et me begin with a simple but provocative statement.

Democracy in America is in large measure gone. The idea that we have a representative democracy, in which candidates raise their own money based on their overall popular support, no longer matches reality. Today, the political system is an unequal, undemocratic system run by and for the powerful, elite few. Special interests have come to dominate, and arguably determine, our elections.

As a result, our two-party system has become so partisan and ideologically inflexible that it no longer has anything to do with the needs of ordinary people.

And because of the Supreme Court's 2010 *Citizens United* decision[1]—which legalized unlimited independent expenditures to support or oppose federal candidates, effectively removing restrictions on political donations by corporations or unions—the power of political money is now greater than ever before.

Citizens United is also directly responsible for the growing impact of "super" political action committees—super PACs—which, thanks to the

Court's decision, can raise unlimited sums from individuals, corporations, unions, and other groups. Super PACs have already corrupted the political system in ways unimaginable just a few years ago.

This huge change has only begun to be recognized by the media, with little coverage of what is considered a technical matter.

The imbalance in the campaign finance system has further isolated voters from politicians and contributed enormously to the deep disenchantment with Congress and Washington. Distrust of our governing institutions has grown to heights never seen in the history of public polling. An ABC News poll in June 2011 found 69 percent described themselves as dissatisfied with or even angry about the way the federal government is working. Fewer than one in five respondents had any confidence left in government.[2]

This distrust is rooted substantially in a conviction that the system has become a casino, not a true democracy. Special-interest money has also exacerbated polarization, not just between the two parties but also within the broader electorate. Because most of the money comes from groups with a strongly ideological cast—whether labor unions on the left or the Club for Growth on the right—candidates are pulled away from the center and toward extreme positions. Special interests have made personal issues—basic individual freedoms like contraception, abortion, and religion—front-page news and have distracted the voters from the critical business of America.

Given the current direction of campaign finance law, it's likely that our political system will grow even more polarized, that the two parties will be even less willing to put forth constructive solutions, and that candidates will be deferential only to their most generous donors—who are, almost invariably, those with the most extreme ideological views, right-wing or left-wing. The ordinary voter, who lacks both ideological commitment and financial clout, is left standing on the sidelines.

Political advertising—especially negative advertising aimed at opposition candidates—has grown considerably in the last few years. And the airwaves will get noisier as checks pour in to the super PACs, the primary engine that finances media buys. A general political rule of thumb is that roughly 70 percent of all money raised in presidential campaigns goes to buying media spots. The overwhelming majority of these are negative, attack ads—and a great many of them are misleading or flat-out inaccurate. Experts predict that the Republicans and Democrats together will raise $2 billion for the 2012 race for the White House. The nasty rhetoric has already ramped up; on the GOP side, we saw it especially during the days leading up to a key caucus or primary. The vitriol in today's campaign advertising is excessive by any measure. And, of course, the incessant ads and robocalls leading up to an actual vote are funded with super PAC money.

Indeed, anyone who looks at campaign 2012 will see that the GOP primaries were determined in large measure by the money that super PACs have given to Mitt Romney, Newt Gingrich, and, to a lesser extent, Rick Santorum and Ron Paul. But the stark reality is that without super PACs, nobody can play in the modern political arena. The price at the turnstile is just too high. This reality, unfortunately, has seeped into the campaigns of state and local elections as well. It won't be long before it will take a multimillion-dollar war chest just to run for a state assembly seat.

Today, money leads and everything else follows. The super PACs strengthened the power of the political class and the insider and beltway elites who work on their own or in concert with party functionaries.

Aides, consultants, and lobbyists have the direct pipeline to policy decisions. The rest of us are pretty much irrelevant.

Two years ago, President Obama took the high road on the dangers of the super PACs. Speaking out in defense of the proposed DISCLOSE Act, which would require corporate political advertisers to name who's funding their activities, Obama said: "A vote to oppose these reforms is nothing less than a vote to allow corporate and special interest takeovers of our elections. It is damaging to our democracy."[3] The legislation stalled in the Senate and Obama expressed disappointment.

But by February 2012, Obama was singing a different tune. His reelection campaign reversed Obama's stance and decided to support Priorities USA,[4] a super PAC attempting to countervail the fundraising efforts of Republican super PACs. The lesson in this story: if you want to be reelected, you don't bring a knife to a gunfight.

Obama's endorsement of Priorities USA—and the lavish spending Republican super PACs did in the 2012 GOP primaries for one candidate or another—should make clear to all that the super PACs' claim of independence is a patent fiction. They are created and run by friends of the candidates, family members of the candidates, former employees of the candidates, longtime fundraisers of the candidates, and business partners of the campaign managers. We would have to be incredibly naïve to think that these people are not in constant touch with one another—or so in "sync" that overt communication is not needed—during the height of a campaign season.

Moreover, an advisory opinion from the Federal Election Commission last year permitted political candidates to attend meetings of donors—potential supporters for these super PACs—and even to endorse their efforts, within certain parameters. Former FEC commissioner and election legal expert Trevor Potter explains: "They can't solicit an unlimited amount of money, but they can go in and say, 'you're doing great work, this is really important to my campaign.' If the message is 'these are my people, I want you to support this group,' then someone can, in fact, go out and write a check for a million dollars. They just can't be directly solicited by the candidate."[5] That's a restriction barely worthy of the name.

So the coffers of super PACs overflow with donations, and the ethical boundaries of campaign financing have now been widened to a point that should embarrass everyone involved in elective politics. Money rules the day in American politics and will continue to do so until the day that Americans collectively demand reform. At the rate things are going, that day needs to come very soon.

●●●●●●●●●

WHAT THIS BOOK IS ABOUT

In March 2012, I sat on a panel for Reuters TV on campaign finance and the impact of *Citizens United*. One panelist was former Louisiana governor Buddy Roemer, who is seeking the presidential nomination of Americans Elect, a nonpartisan group that is conducting the first online presidential nomination process in American history. Roemer pledges to accept donations of no more than $100 per individual. Another panelist was Senator John McCain, who cosponsored the Bipartisan Campaign Reform Act of 2002 with Russ Feingold—a law that was intended to clean up the abuses of money in politics but ended up worsening them, and eventually spurred the *Citizens United* decision.

During the panel discussion, McCain predicted that eventually we would see huge campaign finance scandals involving super PACs. He suggested that it might take just such a scandal to get Americans focused on how political money has distorted our system.

I admire Senator McCain, and I agree with him in the broadest sense about the abuses of super PACs, megadonors, and special interests. But I don't agree that "it will take a scandal."

The system itself is a scandal.

I cannot overstate how dire the situation is. The very foundation of our democracy—free elections—has been deeply damaged and is desperately in need of repair. Unless a national movement arises to radically reform the role of money in politics, the system will likely continue to reward those wealthy individuals who commit large sums to narrow-interest "causes" and candidates equally committed to those causes.

American Casino is not about lamenting the campaign spending misdeeds of one side or the other. Both parties are neck deep in political money, in slightly different ways, as I'll document. I'm not advocating a partisan position.

This book will explore the multiple forces that have led to the capture of both parties, and thus our democratic system, by political money. It will document the individuals and groups that make up this new universe of political money, demonstrate the outsized influence they have attained over the political process, and make clear why this system is so profoundly undemocratic and so needs to change.

Politicians have their eyes on a single issue, first and foremost: raising enough money to get elected or reelected. Big money rules.

Unlimited spending and secret spending now define the campaign finance system in the United States. As Sheila Krumholz, executive director of the Center for Responsive Politics, puts it: "The money has shifted to the fringes and it's become less and less transparent. It's shifting away from the parties, the candidates, the PACs, and shifting to these unregulated groups and becoming much more secret."[6]

The days when candidates raised their own money are long gone. By and large, fundraising—and thus, campaign spending—has become the nearly exclusive preserve of the elite few.

To have any influence on the outcome of a race, you must be a director of a party committee, the executive director of a special-interest PAC or organization, or better yet, a billionaire or multimillionaire. The phrase "special interests" doesn't begin to capture just how concentrated power has become in a few hands in recent years.

While these groups don't represent the broader electorate, they have increasingly vast financial resources, with which they flood PACs, state and national party committees, and individual candidates's campaigns.

In politics today, ideological groups and party committees together form a self-reinforcing, secret establishment that determines the outcome of elections far more than individual candidates do on their own. As one media consultant told me:

> Look, we don't care about the candidates, we don't care about the campaign managers and we certainly don't care about the campaign organizations. What we really care about now are the PACs and the super PACs. We are looking to get the organized big-money groups because that's where the money is, that's where the influence is, and that's where elections are decided.

The newly born super PACs are the most nefarious repositories of campaign cash—and the ultimate weapon that political insiders use to keep the average citizen in the dark. Super PACs give the politicos a new road map to corruption. What's more, most of the money is raised in six- and seven-figure checks from just a few individuals or corporations. The maximum $2,500 individual campaign contribution allowed by law is no longer an encumbrance.

Campaign finance in the United States isn't run by the 1 percenters anymore: it's run by the .0001 percenters. Elected officials at all levels know they cannot keep their jobs unless they prostrate themselves to the elite few who line their campaign coffers.

With the influence of regular Americans being buried by large donations from millionaires, large corporations, and interest groups, a number of PACs and other vehicles of both the left and right have risen in response. They often cast themselves as anti-Washington and anti-business-as-usual, and they've developed some innovative techniques. But at their core, they're principally dedicated to prevailing politically—like any other PAC or interest group—in ways that will serve their parochial interests. If the broad American middle class had the money and organization to compete with these mega-rich elites, the "game" of politics might not be as rigged as a roadside casino. But under the system as it now stands, the American people do not. They are being hoodwinked, ripped off, and defrauded in ways they have not experienced since the early days of the Republic, if not more.

Even those in positions of power seem to recognize the threat that the new world of campaign finance represents. Starbucks CEO Howard Schultz began a campaign to get other company heads to refuse to donate money to politicians until there is substantial reform. A group of about two hundred business executives formed a bipartisan organization calling on companies to be more transparent in their political activity and urging Congress to pass new disclosure laws. Rep. Chris Van Hollen, a Maryland Democrat, has introduced legislation to close gaping loopholes in the disclosure laws. It would require super PACs to immediately disclose their donors and campaign expenditures, and it would mandate that the PACs' top five donors be listed on each of their ads, along with the sums they gave.[7]

Efforts like these are urgently needed. Otherwise, in the words of Trevor Potter, president and general counsel of the Campaign Legal Center and a former FEC chairman: "The whole country is going to see a situation where corporate interests are going to be electing members of Congress"[8] to cater to their needs.

We desperately need to take our democracy off the auction block and put it back in the hands of its citizens, where the founding fathers wanted it to be. Only wholesale, systemic change can address the stranglehold that megadonors, power brokers, and super PACs now have on our political system.

More and more, our system of government operates in the shadows, with little or no say from ordinary Americans. The advent of super PACs is the primary reason.

Let's take a look at where they come from and how they operate.

How Super PACs Changed Everything

"We had a 10-year plan to take all this down," he said. "If we do it right, I think we can pretty well dismantle the entire regulatory regime that is called campaign finance law. . . . We have been awfully successful and we are not done yet."

—James Bopp Jr., *New York Times*, January 25, 2010

While *Citizens United* is perhaps the culmination of developments that have been accelerating over the last decade and a half, there is simply no overstating the magnitude of the decision. Understanding the impact of *Citizens United* requires a basic idea of how political fundraising was conducted in the decades before 2010.

For the past sixty years or so, conventional political action committees (PACs) have been the center of the fundraising universe, generating untold millions for candidates. PACs are essentially legal slush funds for special-interest groups, ranging from the conservative Club for Growth—which raises money for Republican candidates who pledge to support limited government and lower taxes—to the left-leaning feminist group EMILY's List, which works to elect pro-choice Democratic women. PACs enforce orthodoxy in each party and exert enormous influence on campaigns.

There are many different kinds of PACs. One common variety is the leadership PAC—a committee established by a member of Congress to support other political candidates. Leadership PACs, which can accept donations from individuals or other PACs, allow elected officials to set themselves up as kingpins, seeding the campaigns of other candidates and thereby extending their own influence and power. For example, House majority leader Eric Cantor's Every Republican Is Crucial PAC has so far taken in more than $3.5 million for the 2012 election cycle, disbursing $3.3 million of that sum to other candidates in the first half of 2011.[9] A leadership PAC cannot spend money on direct mail or ads to support the campaigns of its sponsor—Cantor must find funding for his own races elsewhere—but leadership PACs may fund travel, administrative expenses, consultants, polling, and other noncampaign expenses.

As potent as these various PACs have been in our recent political history, the super PACs that emerged from the *Citizens United* case and the follow-on decision in *SpeechNow.org v. Federal Election Commission* make them look like twentieth-century weapons in a twenty-first-century war.

By a historic 5-4 vote in *Citizens United v. Federal Election Commission*, the Supreme Court ruled that the government cannot prevent corporations and unions from spending unlimited money to support or criticize specific candidates. The ruling, announced in January 2010, dealt a major blow to the McCain-Feingold law, which sought to limit certain aspects of campaign donations. The full ramifications of the decision will be debated for years, but few dispute that it has made money in politics more central than ever.

Citizens United, a conservative not-for-profit group, had sought to broadcast an unflattering documentary about Hillary Clinton, *Hillary: The Movie*, along with related ads, on television during the 2008 Democratic primaries. The FEC prohibited the broadcasts on the grounds that the movie and ads constituted illegal "electioneering communications" under McCain-Feingold, which barred such groups from even mentioning the name of an elected official in any communications within sixty days of an election.

Citizens United sued the FEC, arguing that such communications qualified as protected speech under the First Amendment. The Court agreed, and in doing so ruled that, under the First Amendment, corporate- or union-sponsored independent political expenditures—that is, spending not coordinated with or directed by a candidate's campaign— *cannot be limited*. A major portion of McCain-Feingold had been overturned.

Two months after the *Citizens United* decision, a federal appeals court ruled in *SpeechNow* that political committees making independent expenditures could accept donations unlimited in size—and that nonprofits could also accept unlimited contributions from corporations and unions, in addition to *unlimited individual contributions*. This put nonprofit political groups in the driver's seat: already free of FEC disclosure requirements, they now had the legal means to accept any amount of money, effectively making it open season for anyone with a political agenda to contribute to these entities. The *SpeechNow* decision also allowed the nonprofits to spend money directly on ads supporting or opposing specific candidates, further undoing the restrictions on campaign fundraising.

Finally, a May 2011 ruling by U.S. district judge James Cacheris struck down the long-standing ban on direct corporate contributions to federal candidates (which *Citizens United* had actually left intact). *Citizens United* and its follow-on rulings have led to a free-for-all in campaign finance, empowering the political elite to funnel even more money into politics with even less transparency than ever before.

The 2010 rulings were the capstone of a three-decade legal effort to eradicate the limits on election spending. They represented a crowning victory for a sixty-three-year-old conservative midwestern lawyer, James Bopp Jr., with a long résumé of litigation challenging campaign finance regulations. Of the thirty-one lawsuits tracked by the Washington-based Campaign Legal Center, Bopp has filed twenty-one—including *Citizens United*.

"It's safe to say that groups on the left and right have Jim Bopp to thank for their newfound freedom," says Sheila Krumholz, a campaign finance analyst. Adds Scott Thomas, a former Democratic FEC chairman: "We should now call the statute, 'The Federal Election Campaign Act paid for and authorized by Jim Bopp.' " Thomas and others contend that Bopp's cases have all but gutted the well-intentioned 2002 McCain-Feingold law, which attempted to rein in outside groups and weaken the influence of wealthy donors.

Overnight, *Citizens United* became the politician's dream and the voter's nightmare—wresting power and influence from millions of ordinary voters and consolidating it within a small circle of big-business power players and other monied interests. *Citizens United* makes campaign finance compliance even murkier and further limits public information about political money. It allows corporations, unions, and associations to report their donors to the Federal Election Commission on a monthly or quarterly basis, meaning that they can make expenditures without immediate, full disclosure of the source of the funds. This all but guarantees that campaign finance machinations won't be discovered until well after a victorious candidate has been sworn into office.

By allowing corporations and independent groups to raise unlimited amounts to promote candidates, *Citizens United* and its follow-on rulings opened up the floodgates to a new universe of campaign finance.

● ● ● ● ● ● ● ●

HOW SUPER PACS WORK

Landon Rowland, a director and chairman emeritus of the Janus Capital Group, aptly described our current campaign finance system: "Substitution of the rule of cash for the rule of law."[10]

The process is now fairly linear and crystal clear. First, take a stance on a big third-rail issue: abortion, taxes, government spending, religion, health care, or the environment, for example. Second, form a super PAC (it's pretty easy to do). Third, find deep-pocket donors that support a candidate's position on one of those items and get them to fund the super PAC. Fourth, spend the money in negative advertising that denigrates the opposing political candidate. It's all legal, and you can do it with shell corporations that completely hide where the money is coming from.

Technically, super PACs operate under few restraints—except that they must disclose the source of their contributions to the FEC and they cannot coordinate directly with candidates or political parties.

Candidates must not "request, suggest, or assent" to an ad run by a super PAC on their behalf. If that doesn't sound like much of a restraint, it's because it's not. "Everyone understands they're functioning as arms of the candidate's campaign," said Fred Wertheimer, the founder of Democracy 21. "Their whole purpose is to circumvent the contribution limits—so we end up with a system of legalized bribery."[11]

Of course, money has always played a significant role in American elections. But the order of the process used to go the other way: first came the candidate; then came the issue (or sometimes the issue and candidate came together); and then, and only then, came the money.

Back when I was starting out in political work, candidates for president and Congress relied on campaign donations within specified limits. Some readers may recall that in the 1970s, there were slush funds and illegal campaign contributions, many ultimately revealed during the Watergate scandal. New York Yankees owner George Steinbrenner was convicted on felony charges because he ordered employees to make contributions to President Nixon's reelection campaign fund and then reimbursed them in kind. It was one way to circumvent the limit, albeit flatly illegal. Today, there's no need for these kinds of acts. The courts have basically sanctioned this behavior.

Undisclosed nonprofit spending, or what has been called "dark money," exploded immediately after the *Citizens United* ruling. Just 53 percent of nonparty outside spending was disclosed in 2011.[12] Assume that the other half of the spending wasn't disclosed to protect the nonprofits from potential embarrassment. (In February 2012, seven Democratic senators sent a letter to the IRS calling for an investigation into social-welfare nonprofits that spend large amounts on direct political advertising. It's not clear whether a potential probe will have any effect on unfettered campaign financing—but if it does, it won't be until *after* the 2012 races.)

Topping it all off, super PACs can skirt the disclosure requirements themselves by accepting donations from those same nondisclosing nonprofits. They can say their money came from a 501(c)(4) group (a kind of nonprofit advocacy group), which is true on its face—but where did the 501(c)(4) group's money come from? They're not obligated to tell.

During the 2010 midterm elections, these independent groups functioned effectively as unregulated party committees—eighty-four super PACs funneled billions of dollars into campaign advertisements, including more than $65 million in reported expenditures to a wide range of candidates.

Super PACs are typified by organizations like American Crossroads, a conservative group spearheaded by Karl Rove, the former top strategist for George W. Bush, and former Republican National Committee chairman Ed Gillespie. Formed in 2010, American Crossroads initially reported its activities to the IRS as a so-called 527 organization (yet another kind of nonprofit advocacy organization). After the *SpeechNow* ruling, American Crossroads registered with the FEC as an independent-expenditure-only committee, better known as a super PAC. Steven Law, who heads the group, worked in George W. Bush's Labor Department and served as Senator Mitch McConnell's chief of staff. He was also the executive director of the National Republican Senatorial Committee and served as the U.S. Chamber of Commerce's general counsel.

American Crossroads regularly discloses its donors—but Crossroads Grassroots Policy Strategies, a spinoff registered with the IRS as a 501(c)(4) nonprofit group, does not. Crossroads GPS, which has donor anonymity because it claims "social-welfare" nonprofit status,[13] has consistently outraised its super PAC sister. In 2011, largely because of donor anonymity, Crossroads GPS raised $31.6 million; American Crossroads raised only $18.4 million in disclosed funds.[14] The nonprofit spent $26 million on issue ads in 2011 targeting President Obama and various members of Congress, according to a *Huffington Post* review of Crossroads GPS press releases.

All of these organizational layers can make the money flowchart difficult to comprehend—and that's precisely the idea.

What does it take to start a super PAC? Apparently not very much. First, you have to open a bank account and file a statement of organization with the FEC listing an address, a treasurer, and the name and address of the bank. Then, another letter must be sent to the FEC indicating that the PAC will be run in a fashion consistent with *Citizens United* and the relevant FEC advisory opinion. After that, it's up to you to work the phones to get people to donate. With the ease of entry and the rollback of contribution limits, affluent individuals are eager to get into the donation game.

In February 2010, Bill Maher, the unabashedly left-wing host of HBO's popular political comedy show *Real Time*, made a $1 million donation to the super PAC Priorities USA Action because he felt that President Obama would be undermanned and underfunded as large Republican donations rolled in. Unlike Stephen Colbert, who started his own super

PAC to satirize the system, Maher regarded his donation more seriously. "I promise you, when it comes to election night, it's going to be neck and neck," he said. "It's going to be a very tight race."[15]

Maher and Colbert are high-profile entertainers who wanted people to know about their super PAC activities. But what's really striking about most super PACs is their opaqueness. Those wishing to conceal their identities when donating to a super PAC may do so easily by contributing through a limited liability corporation (LLC), which must provide only a name and an address. These can be structured in a way that further conceals the identity of the donor.

For example, Restore Our Future, the prominent pro–Mitt Romney super PAC, received a $250,000 donation from one Glenbrook LLC, which listed its address as Lagoon Drive in Redwood City, California. The address matches that of a public accounting firm, Seiler LLP, which refuses to discuss its clients. Who gave that quarter of a million? There's no legal way to find out. There are also eight Glenbrook LLCs registered throughout the country, of which only one is registered with the California secretary of state, and that particular Glenbrook denies any connection to the donation.[16]

Restore Our Future accepted another $250,000 donation from Paumanok Partners LLC, which listed only a post office box outside of New Canaan, Connecticut, in campaign finance records. There is a Paumanok Partners LLC registered with the New York secretary of state, however, and the address it provided—in East Northport, Long Island—is home to nearly a dozen corporations, none of them Paumanok Partners LLC.[17] (Not everyone requires secrecy, of course. The respective donations of Foster Friess and Sheldon Adelson to the Red White and Blue Fund and

Winning Our Future super PACs were well-known to the press and public. But officially they were largely undisclosed and concealed by the PACs.)

FEC filing system requirements also contribute to the hidden nature of super PACs, keeping voters in the dark for as long as possible.

Donations made in January must be disclosed in January, but the filing can be done on the last day of the month. This meant that voters in New Hampshire's 2012 presidential primary didn't know until a month after the polls closed who made the final donations influencing their election. For example, it was not until three weeks after the primary that voters learned John Huntsman's father had donated $1.9 million to his Our Destiny super PAC. The origin of most of the $5.5 million raised through year's end for the pro–Rick Perry Make Us Great Again super PAC was only discovered after the governor dropped out of the presidential race.[18] Donations spent in the Iowa, New Hampshire, South Carolina, and Florida primaries weren't made public until after those states had voted.[19] (I discuss the 2012 GOP primaries in detail in Chapter 5.)

Today, it doesn't take a nimble mind to understand how to advance a candidate (or denigrate another) by deploying capital to circumvent the intent of the law. Political advertisements considered "issue advocacy" steer clear of calling for the election or defeat of a candidate, instead presenting negative cases against the candidates as they relate to issues. The court's ruling said an ad qualifies as express advocacy only if it "explicitly" calls for viewers to vote for or against a particular candidate.

Super PACs can meet that standard, even while running the harshest negative ads.

●●●●●●●●●

SUPER PACS AND NEGATIVE ADVERTISING

The final link in the chain of campaign funding is the expenditures themselves—where and on what the money is spent. Ultimately, the money raised is parceled out by political consultants who have carefully and expertly analyzed the proper media buys for their candidates. These consultants invest in focus groups, polling, and other surveys to determine the zip codes, ethnic backgrounds, and every pertinent element of psychographic and demographic profiling from their databases. They know precisely when and where to target their campaign spending efforts.

A huge portion of super PAC money goes to TV advertising, billboards, and last-minute robocalls to influence voters' decisions. Of course, super PAC money cannot be used to advocate specifically *for* a given candidate; so the money is spent on influencing people to vote *against* the candidate's opponent.

Colloquially, these are known as "negative spots." They've been around a long time. Nobody really likes them, not even those who produce them. But everyone knows that they work.

The psychology behind them is simple. People understand that all the candidates have inherent flaws. They know that the media will spend an inordinate amount of time and resources to expose these flaws. When voters go into a booth undecided, their mind immediately drifts to the candidate they feel carries the least baggage. It is human nature to vote *against* someone you dislike strongly rather than to vote *for* the candidate you like only somewhat.

The first negative ad of the modern era—when TV became the critical medium for elective politics—appeared in 1964. Called the "Daisy" ad, it was the brainchild of Tony Schwartz, a New Yorker who started his career as a graphic designer. He collaborated with the Doyle Dane Bernbach ad agency to create a TV spot featuring a freckled little girl counting aloud as she pulled the petals from a daisy in a bucolic meadow. The scene then changed into a countdown to a mushroom cloud. The implication was clear: vote for President Lyndon Johnson's challenger, Senator Barry Goldwater, and risk the possibility of nuclear war. The ad concluded with Johnson's own voice-over saying: "We must either love each other or we must die."

The ad made no mention of Goldwater (which under today's rules would make it a legal super PAC ad). After a public outcry, it was withdrawn after only a single broadcast. Many people remember the ad; few know that it ran only once—but once was enough. Johnson was reelected in a landslide, and the ad is regarded as the father of all negative political advertising.rea

Democratic presidential candidates have tried but failed to duplicate the Johnson ad's success. In 1984, former vice president Walter Mondale ran a negative ad suggesting that if President Reagan were reelected, we would need to dig bomb shelters. The ad backfired, however, because it occurred four years too late. Democrats had suggested in 1980 that Reagan might have a quick nuclear trigger finger, but he exhibited no such behavior during his first term. He was not willing to bargain with the Soviet Union, but he wasn't threatening them by opening the missile silos, either. Mondale lost to Reagan in one of the most lopsided elections in American history.

The infamous "Willie Horton" spot is probably the most influential negative political ad of the last thirty years. Produced during the 1988 presidential campaign, the ad was paid for by a political group officially acting separately from the campaign of Vice President George H. W. Bush, who was running against Michael Dukakis, then governor of Massachusetts. Jane Mayer of *The New Yorker* later called it the "equivalent of an improvised explosive device."[20]

The ad's key image was a mug shot of Horton, who was black, scowling at the police camera. A convicted murderer, Horton had escaped while on a weekend pass issued by a Massachusetts furlough program. He raped a white woman and stabbed her fiancé. The ad was designed to make voters worry that Dukakis, who had vetoed a bill a decade earlier that would have ended furloughs for convicted murderers, was soft on crime. Causing a racial firestorm, the Horton ad went a long way toward dismantling the Democratic campaign for the White House.[21] Bush beat Dukakis decisively.

In addition to its racial overtones—which both Democrats and Republicans condemned—the Horton ad was important for another reason, one very relevant to today. It "raised unsettling new questions about possibly unlawful coordination between an official campaign and an outside political group," wrote Mayer in *The New Yorker*. "In retrospect, the spot was not an aberration; both in its tone and in its murky origins, it created a blueprint for the future."[22]

Two decades later, super PACs—both in their tactics and their thinly disguised, if unofficial, coordination with the campaigns—have perfected the blueprint.

During the 2004 presidential race, the Swift Boat Veterans for Truth produced a memorable attack on the Democratic candidate, John Kerry.

The vets first held a press conference in May challenging Kerry's Vietnam War service record. Three months later, the group produced TV ads. On August 5, 2004, they began airing a one-minute spot in three swing states. Entitled "Any Questions?" the ad was a collage of short clips of thirteen Swift Boaters, many of whom said they "served with John Kerry" or had direct contact with him during his tour in Southeast Asia. The veterans claimed that Kerry was dishonest, unreliable, and unfit to lead and had dishonored his country and fellow veterans. As it turned out, only one of the men in the ad had actually served under Kerry; some sailed alongside Kerry's Swift Boat on multiboat patrols. Eight years later, the veracity of the Swift Boat ads is still a matter of debate. (See Chapter 2 for more on the role of the Swift Boat ads in the 2004 campaign.)

Today, there appear to be no lengths to which campaigns will not go in stretching the boundaries of truth. A political operative for Mitt Romney's 2012 campaign who wished to remain anonymous put it this way: "First of all, ads are propaganda by definition. We are in the persuasion business, the propaganda business. . . . Ads are agitprop. . . . Ads are about hyperbole, they are about editing. It's ludicrous for them to say that an ad is taking something out of context. . . . All ads do that. They are manipulative pieces of persuasive art."[23]

That sounds like an elegant way of saying: anything goes.

The huge database of political speeches and off-the-cuff utterances can be edited and tailored to convey almost any message. Campaigns continually scan these archives for sound bites that can be used to attack an opponent. Consider the speech Barack Obama gave on October 16, 2008, while campaigning in Londonderry, New Hampshire. Speaking a month after the financial collapse that saw stock prices plunge and many Americans lose large portions of their savings in retirement plans, Obama said that his opponent, John McCain, didn't have his finger on the pulse of Middle America's problems. Obama pilloried McCain's lack of understanding of the full impact of the world fiscal crisis: "Senator McCain's campaign actually said, and I quote, 'If we keep talking about the economy, we're going to lose.'"

An innocent enough comment, to be sure. But three years later, it came back to haunt Obama in a campaign ad. How? In 2011, Romney's campaign edited the Londonderry remark into an ad, disregarding the plain fact that Obama was quoting someone else—the words of a McCain staffer. The Romney ad made it sound like Obama was talking about his *own* campaign in saying, "If we keep talking about the economy, we're going to lose"—thus making it appear that Obama was admitting culpability for all the economic ills during his first three years in office. The nonpartisan website Politifact.com, which evaluates the accuracy of political ads, was being charitable when it called the Romney ad "ridiculously misleading" and gave it its worst rating: Pants on Fire.[24]

But such is the power of super PACs, unregulated contributions, and faceless, anonymous donors that we can expect to see a lot more of these kinds of efforts.

To make clear just how corrosive the new campaign finance framework has become and how influential—even dispositive—it has become of election outcomes, we need to look back. Five election cycles—2004, 2006, 2008, 2010, and now 2012—demonstrate the destructive impact of money on U.S. politics. Each election cycle had its own unique characteristics and factors, but all shared one trait in common: in each, the role of money was more pervasive and more powerful than the election before.

The election cycle that set us on the road to *Citizens United* was 2004—the first campaign, ironically, to take place *after* the landmark McCain-Feingold campaign finance reform bill. It was 2004 that saw the first explosion of the independent-expenditure groups operating in the loopholes of that federal legislation—the forerunners of today's super PACs.

2

Swift-Boating the System:
The 2004 Elections

Although the 527 committees have been operating on the fringes of American politics for at least the past three election cycles, election 2004 was the first time they played a major role, perhaps a decisive role, in determining the outcome of a national election.

—Center for Public Integrity, December 2004[25]

Of all the subplots in the presidential election, none were as sorry as the Democrats' pioneering "527" groups—named for the section of the tax code that governs them. The 527s were intended to circumvent the law's strictures against having unlimited soft money flood into political races. The Democrats built these new shadow-party advocacy groups to attack the president early in the campaign season and build voter-turnout

machines. Then they watched Bush partisans adapt the same financing
device to float the campaign's most notorious and devastating attack ads,
the Swift boat assaults on John Kerry's heroic war record and his antiwar
activities after he returned from Vietnam.

—*New York Times*, December 29, 2004

I n 2007, the *Wall Street Journal* reported that "Over the past four years, the national Democratic and Republican parties have raised and spent less on elections than during the prior four years, when adjusted for inflation. At the same time, independent political groups have more than doubled their spending, and have begun to rival the parties as an election-season financial force."[26]

That trend got underway with the 2004 elections, the first to take place after the passage of the Bipartisan Campaign Reform Act of 2002, popularly known as McCain-Feingold after its sponsors. The law was mainly concerned with cracking down on "soft-money" donations to political parties and candidates by corporations, unions, and individuals—and in this goal it proved largely successful.

However, in the best tradition of unintended consequences, McCain-Feingold set off a money race through alternate channels—primarily through tax-exempt, outside political organizations known as 527s—that would very quickly transform the landscape of campaign finance forever. By discouraging giving directly to political parties and candidates, McCain-Feingold made 527s a much more attractive option—since these groups were, officially at least, independent and not affiliated with parties or candidates. In 2004, 527 groups would receive $405 million in contributions, up from only $151 million in 2002.[27] Meanwhile, party soft-money donations fell by $337 million.[28]

Though 527s were barred from expressly advocating the election or defeat of specific candidates or parties, they operated otherwise, by and large, outside of campaign-finance law. They could advocate based on issues, and they could identify candidates—negatively or positively—in connection with these issues so long as they didn't urge a specific course of action from the voters. Although 527s had been around since 1975, they hadn't been important players in U.S. elections until the 1990s, with the growth in issue-based campaigns. Now, they stepped to the forefront of U.S. politics.

What happened in 2004, in sum, was this: Democrats, eager to take back the White House and deeply concerned about George W. Bush's fundraising prowess and the traditional advantages of incumbency, set out to find outside funding for the 2004 campaign. While Republican success in 2004 led many to assume that the GOP had pioneered 527 groups, in fact, Democrats got there first. They took the early lead in the innovative use of 527 organizations, raising vast sums of cash through the financial assistance of several super-wealthy individuals and the cutting-edge participation of their 527 groups. The Democratic 527s funded a spring offensive of political advertising that helped put John Kerry ahead in early polling. At the presidential level, Kerry-supporting 527s outspent Bush-supporting 527s by a whopping 3-to-1 margin: $188 million to $62 million.[29] (See Fig. 2-1.)

Democrats have retained a funding advantage among 527 groups, in fact, up to the present day. Yet their financial advantages weren't enough to deliver the 2004 election and the White House. Why not?

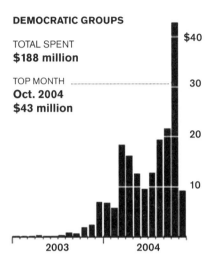

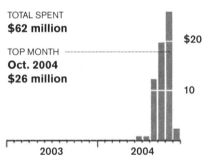

The New York Times

The evidence suggests the following: first, the Republicans caught on, caught up, and soon mastered the 527-driven issue-advertising campaign. Their greatest success came in late summer and early fall with the media presence of the Swift Boat Veterans for Truth, an independent-expenditure group whose ads did so much damage to Kerry's presidential campaign by calling into question his service in Vietnam.

Second—and most important—the Democratic and Republican 527 groups allocated their resources very differently. The Democratic groups in many cases front-loaded their investments, while the Republican groups did not. And the Democratic groups split their monies down the homestretch between voter-outreach campaigns and media buys, while the Republican 527 almost exclusively focused their resources on the media campaign. At a crucial point in the campaign—just as the Swift Boaters were doing real damage—key Democratic 527s like The Media Fund and MoveOn.org ran short of cash.

The Swift Boat campaign was devastating to Kerry and may well have been the decisive moment in the 2004 race. As it is, he lost the presidency by only by a 100,000-vote margin in Ohio, so it shouldn't require much beyond common sense to understand how different the outcome might have been with a more effective Democratic 527 media strategy in the campaign's crucial autumn months.

So the 2004 race was, in effect, a story of two 527 campaigns: the first leg won by the Democrats and the second and decisive one won by the Republicans. When it was all over, the Republicans had retained the White House and both houses of Congress. Democratic bitterness over the results led to a resolve not to let the same thing happen next time; thus, 2004 was only the opening salvo in a new round of outside-group spending wars in American politics. These groups have spent more and more each cycle, right up to 2012—which will be the most expensive campaign season in American history.

The 2004 campaign showed another crucial characteristic about outside-group participation: the 527s were predominantly an instrument of the super-wealthy. As the Campaign Finance Institute reported: "Most ($256 million) of the $405 million in contributions to federal 527s in '04 came from individuals."[30] Political money has always been an important part of our system; but now so much more money is needed to compete, and the sources of that money are increasingly confined to elites and the wealthiest, most powerful individuals in the United States. CFI went on to predict, with foresight, that "the preponderance of large donors is likely to raise—even more seriously than it does now—the question of what the BCRA [Bipartisan Campaign Reform Act] has really accomplished."[31]

Actually, what the BCRA has accomplished—along with the *Citizens United* ruling of 2010—is quite clear: the end of democratic elections in the United States and the advent of a new system run by and for super elites and political insiders.

● ● ● ● ● ● ●

THE DEMOCRATS GET OUT OF THE BLOCKS FIRST

The McCain-Feingold legislation passed in November 2002 and went into effect on January 1, 2003. Democrats seemed to understand before Republicans did that the new law, while imposing major restrictions on party fundraising, would also open up new avenues for bringing in campaign cash. Then-party chair Terry McAuliffe and former White House deputy chief of staff Harold Ickes spearheaded an effort to set up 527 organizations and find donors—especially large donors.[32] Three would lead the pack:

- ⍦ **George Soros**, the investor and philanthropist, donated $27 million to 527s in 2004, making him the largest single donor.[33] He played a pivotal role in providing seed money for most of the major Democratic 527s.
- ⍦ **Peter Lewis**, former CEO and current chairman of the Progressive Insurance Company. Lewis donated just under $24 million and matched Soros's contributions to America Coming Together ($10 million) and MoveOn.org ($2.5 million).[34]
- ⍦ **Stephen Bing**, the founder of the Shangri-la business group, made $13.9 million in donations.[35]

These top three individual donors to Democratic groups were also the top three donors overall in 2004, giving roughly $65 million and far outpacing their Republican counterparts.[36] With their help, Democratic 527s would go on to outspend their Republican rivals by the staggering sum of $321 million to $84 million in 2004—a nearly 4-to-1 margin.[37] Ickes and McAuliffe's efforts to get an early jump on 527s had paid off. Their work culminated in the formation of America Coming Together (ACT) and The Media Fund, the two largest 527s during the 2004 campaign season.[38]

The three key Democratic groups in 2004 were:

- ⍦ America Coming Together. With total expenditures of $78

million, ACT dedicated most of its efforts to get-out-the-vote drives. Its largest contributors were Soros and Lewis.[39] ACT was the largest member of America Votes, a broad coalition of left-wing groups including the Sierra Club, EMILY's List, NARAL, Service Employees International Union, and many others.

ര The Media Fund. ACT's sister 527, dedicated to media and issue ads, spent nearly $58 million in 2004, with $48 million going toward advertising. All but one of its TV, radio, and print ads in 2004 were entirely negative.[40]

ര MoveOn.org. MoveOn is perhaps the most enduring 527 to come of age in 2004, with total expenditures of more than $21 million. All but one of its ads were entirely negative.[41] After Republican-leaning 527s began funding the damaging ads sponsored by Swift Boat Veterans for Truth, MoveOn helped set up a Democratic answer group, Texans for Truth, which aired ads questioning President Bush's National Guard record.[42]

●●●●●●●

THE REPUBLICANS RESPOND

For various reasons, the Republicans were slow out of the 527 gate—and in fact, the RNC initially asked the Federal Election Commission to limit the influence of 527s. While Democrats were busy exploring the 527 possibilities, Republicans chose to focus their efforts on a 501(c)(4) nonprofit, Progress for America—which, under that legal designation, was prohibited from having electioneering as a primary purpose.[43] When the FEC didn't take action, the Republicans decided it was time to join the

527 game. In May 2004, Progress for America began organizing a 527 arm.

Despite their slow start, Republicans may, in the end, have gotten more for their money in 2004. While Democratic 527s far outspent their rivals overall, Republicans reversed that ratio toward the later part of the campaign in some crucial areas. In the month before the election, Republican groups spent $29.7 million on broadcast media, according to the Center for Public Integrity, compared with $10.3 million spent by Democratic groups.[44] Figure 2-2 highlights this 3-to-1 disparity in the last three weeks of the campaign.

Figure 2-2

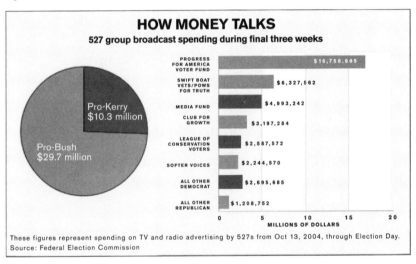

HOW MONEY TALKS

527 group broadcast spending during final three weeks

These figures represent spending on TV and radio advertising by 527s from Oct 13, 2004, through Election Day.
Source: Federal Election Commission

While the top three individual donors to Republican groups gave nearly $19 million—less than a third as much as the $65 million given by the top three Democrats[45]—the two largest Republican donors both gave heavily to Swift Boat Veterans for Truth, giving them a legitimate claim to having had a significant influence over the outcome.[46] The top three Republican 527 donors were:

ᘓ Bob. J. Perry, the owner of Perry Homes, a Texas homebuilding company. Perry gave $8 million in total donations to Republican 527s in 2004—$4.4 million of that going to the Swift Boat Vets.[47][48] Perry had been a longtime contributor to George W. Bush, and in the years to come, he would become a major player in funding Republican super PACs.[49]

ᘓ T. Boone Pickens, the energy magnate, better known in recent years for his Pickens Plan to wean America off foreign oil through the use of wind farms and exploitation of natural gas resources, was the second-largest contributor to Republican 527s.[50] Pickens gave $5.6 million in total donations and $2 million to the Swift Boat Vets, donating partly through his hedge fund BP Capital.[51]

ᘓ Alex Spanos, a real-estate developer and founder of A. G. Spanos Companies, gave a total of $5 million to Progress for America.[52]

There were two key Republican 527 players in 2004:

ᘓ Progress for America Voter Fund (PFA's 527 arm) spent nearly $36 million in the 2004 campaign, including $29 million on advertising.[53] In the last three weeks of the election, PFA outspent the top Democratic group, The Media Fund, by a 3-to-1 margin.[54] This expenditure included a $14 million ad buy for "Ashley's Story," which provided a touching account of Bush's encounter with the daughter of a woman who died on 9/11. The ad was particularly notable for its positive message, a rarity among 527 ads.[55]

୧ Swift Boat Vets and POWs for Truth spent $22.5 million, including $18 million on TV advertising. The group became by far the most famous (or infamous) of the 527 groups.

The ads themselves, which began airing in August 2004, featured "Swift Boat" veterans of Vietnam who had served under John Kerry (or claimed to have done so) questioning both his wartime record and his actions when he returned home.[56] One after another, they called into question the Kerry campaign's narrative of the senator's war heroism:

GEORGE ELLIOTT: John Kerry has not been honest about what happened in Vietnam.

AL FRENCH: He is lying about his record.

LOUIS LETSON: I know John Kerry is lying about his first Purple Heart because I treated him for that injury.

VAN O'DELL: John Kerry lied to get his bronze star. . . . I know, I was there, I saw what happened.

JACK CHENOWETH: His account of what happened and what actually happened are the difference between night and day.

ADMIRAL HOFFMAN: John Kerry has not been honest.

ADRIAN LONSDALE: And he lacks the capacity to lead.

LARRY THURLOW: When the chips were down, you could not count on John Kerry.

BOB ELDER: John Kerry is no war hero.

GRANT HIBBARD: He betrayed all his shipmates . . . he lied before the Senate.

SHELTON WHITE: John Kerry betrayed the men and women he served with in Vietnam.

JOE PONDER: He dishonored his country . . . he most certainly did.[57]

The Swift Boat ad campaign became perhaps the most influential political commercial since the Willie Horton ads of 1988. Many credit these ads, and Kerry's ineffective response, with Bush's eventual victory.

HOW IT PLAYED OUT IN ELECTION 2004

The 2004 presidential race was about as close as they come: Bush won 50.7 percent to 48.3 percent in the popular vote and captured just 286 electoral votes. The 527 groups played a major role in both parties' efforts, but in the end, their effects were felt most in different areas: for the Democratic 527s, in voter mobilization and turnout drives, led by America Coming Together; for the Republican 527s, in the ad wars, led by the Swift Boat Vets.

America Coming Together spent $10 million on Election Day alone for canvassers and field operations.[58] According to one report, ACT became the largest employer in Ohio on Election Day and spent $15 million in the state overall.[59][60] In Florida, ACT spent $10 million and its canvassers visited a quarter-million homes.[61] These efforts undoubtedly kept Kerry close in these states—he lost them both narrowly—and probably helped him win Pennsylvania, where ACT also invested heavily.

Meanwhile, on the Republican side, the RNC executed its own formidable "ground game," geared toward maximizing the Republican base turnout. That left the Republican 527 groups to focus on the media wars, and in the campaign's final weeks, they had far more funding for media than their Democratic counterparts. In fact, according to FEC filings, over the campaign's final *five* months, Republican media-oriented 527s raised nearly twice as much as their Democratic rivals—$69.2 million to $34.8 million. The advantage was particularly pronounced in the third quarter, when the groups were making their media buys for the campaign's final month: Republican groups raised $40 million to the Democrats' $20 million.

During the campaign's final month, MoveOn.org—the most aggressive liberal 527 and a vital organ for Democratic campaign rhetoric and advocacy—saw its receipts fall to nearly zero, at a time when the Swift Boat Vets had no funding problems.

This may, ultimately, tell the story of the 527s in the 2004 campaign: down the stretch, when it counted most, Republican 527s involved in media messaging were much better funded than the Democratic groups. Figure 2-3 following makes clear the funding disparity: it shows the cash flow for the key 527s involved in broadcast ads in the campaign—Progress for America and The Swift Boat Vets for Republicans, The Media Fund and MoveOn.org for the Democrats.[62]

The story comes down to a Democratic advantage in gross donations—tallied up from the beginning of the election cycle, and going back to 2003—but a disparity in the Republicans' favor on when and where those donations were given, and how they were spent. As Figure 2-4 shows, Republican donors like Perry, Pickens, and Spanos were quiet in early 2004, while the big Democratic donors (Soros, Lewis, Bing) gave far more in 2003 and the first half of 2004. Almost all of this money was spent by mid-2004, however. In the second half of the campaign, key Democrats and Republicans gave roughly the same amount—but they didn't allocate the funds in the same way.

Figure 2-3

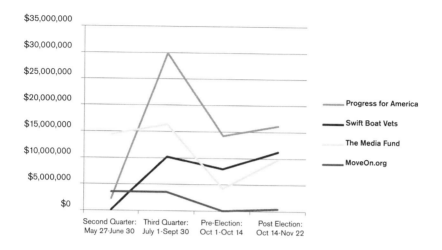

Figure 2-4

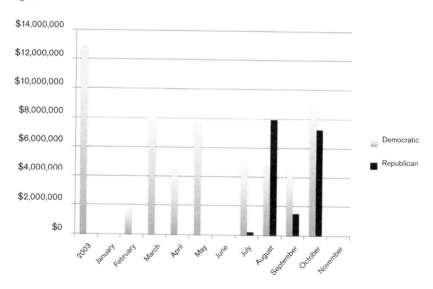

The Democratic 527s were more dedicated to get-out-the-vote efforts, leaving less to spend on media, while Republican 527 funding went almost entirely to advertising. Most of the Democratic donations listed above were given to the Joint Victory Campaign 2004, which then split its funding between America Coming Together and The Media Fund. George Soros contributed $7.5 million directly to ACT—but ACT's efforts were focused on ground-game, voter-turnout efforts. While ACT had plenty of money, The Media Fund had significantly less money available to it than did Progress for America.

Moveon.org fared even worse: while Soros, Lewis, and Bing gave roughly $6 million in total to MoveOn, most of their funding was given—and spent— in the first half of the campaign. Meanwhile, the Swift Boat Vets received a surge of funding at just the point when MoveOn.org ran out of money. Perry and Pickens gave roughly $6.5 million in total to the Swift Boat Vets in the second half of the campaign, and a number of other major donors also contributed during that time.

Given the fact that many attribute Bush's win in 2004 to his campaign's disciplined messaging, it's difficult to overlook the role of Republican 527s, and their heavy emphasis on advertising, in carrying the president to reelection.

CONCLUSION

In its angry end-of-year editorial, in which it looked back on the 2004 campaign, the *New York Times* summarized the 527 story well:

Dollar-wise, the Democrats proved better at milking the 527 strategy, spending more than three times as much as the Republicans in stealth-party ads favoring their presidential ticket. But the Republicans wielded their ads like a rapier once the Federal Election Commission, true to its track record, shirked its responsibility by deciding that the new breed of advocacy groups should not be controlled under the campaign finance reform laws.[63]

More important, as the *Times* pointed out, the Democrats were not emerging from their bitter experience with anything like reform on their minds. On the contrary: their resolve, as they looked ahead to 2006, was to ensure that this time, they sustained their 527 efforts—media efforts included—all the way to Election Day, and that they not allow the Republicans to snatch victory from them at the eleventh hour.

The 2004 election was the inaugural contest in our new campaign finance landscape. From here, each succeeding election cycle would involve more money, more brazen activities from shadowy outside groups—and more financial involvement from those whom Tom Wolfe once described as the masters of the universe. While John Kerry was swift-boated in 2004, it is the rest of us—figuratively speaking, of course—who've been getting swift-boated ever since.

3

Democratic Muscle: Outside Money in 2006 and 2008

Political groups unaffiliated with the two major parties account for an increasingly large share of spending on federal campaigns—19% of the total in 2006, up from just 7% in 2000, according to an analysis of campaign finance data by The Wall Street Journal. They now are horning in on crucial campaign activities once dominated by the parties, such as buying ads and getting out the vote.

Brody Mullins, *Wall Street Journal,* December 19, 2007

SEIU is on the field, it's in the White House, it's in the administration.

—Andy Stern, president, Service Employees International Union[64]

There can be little question, given the closeness of the 2004 race, that the GOP-oriented 527 groups—exemplified by the ad campaign of the Swift Boat Veterans for Truth—played a decisive role in the Republican victory. Many tend to assume that such groups were a Republican invention—but as we have seen, the opposite is true. It was Democrats who got out of the gate first with 527 groups and set the pace for the campaign. Once they caught on, Republicans fought back with a vengeance, particularly in media advertising, and they ended up using the Democrats' innovations against them, beating them at their own game.

In 2006, Democrats were determined not to let the same thing happen. Just as the Republicans had turned their own tool against them, they returned the favor in the midterm elections. Democratic-leaning 527s dominated political spending in 2006 and outspent GOP-oriented groups, $233 million to $154 million.[65]

Of that portion, labor unions gave $42 million,[66] the majority to Democrats running for House and Senate seats. Among a range of other powerful outside spending groups, organized labor would lead the charge in one of the most smashing election years in recent Democratic history, recapturing both the House and the Senate, along with a majority of governorships and state legislatures, from the Republicans.

THE 2006 ELECTIONS

To get an idea of the powerful role that these outside political groups played in 2006—and how, increasingly, they are replacing the parties themselves as the go-to sources of political money—consider that

Republican Party committees outspent Democratic Party committees, $115 million to $108 million. Clearly, a funding advantage at the party level no longer sufficed to win. And it's certainly true that the political landscape was well aligned for Democrats in 2006, with widespread dissatisfaction over the war in Iraq, Republican scandals, and plummeting approval ratings for President George W. Bush and his party generally.

But there was another factor: the role of independent-expenditure groups. A multitude of these groups went to work in the 2006 cycle for Democratic and Republican candidates, but as indicated above, the Democratic-leaning groups held the strong edge.

In a number of House and Senate races, a Republican incumbent's official campaign outraised that of his Democratic opponent, in some races by a margin nearly as dramatic as 2 to 1. Yet outside spending bolstered the efforts of underfunded Democratic challengers and allowed them to compete with, and often defeat, incumbent Republicans.

Standing above all other groups was the hard-core left-wing union Service Employees International Union, "the fastest-growing union in North America."[67] The SEIU represents 2.2 million workers, the majority employed in health care, government, and property management.[68] In addition to representing workers, the SEIU works diligently to preserve labor interests in government. In November 2006, the *National Journal* ranked SEIU as having the most political clout of any major national interest group: in the 2006 election, candidates supported by the union in close races had a win-loss record of 10–4.[69]

While the union itself is authorized to spend political money, it also formed its own 527—and for my purposes here, when I write of SEIU, I'm talking about the union's 527 arm, which outpaced all other

Table 3-1 Federal 527 Organizations Raising or Spending $200,000 or More in 2005-06 Cycle

Organization Name	Contributions Received	Expenditures	Associated PAC
DEMOCRATIC ORIENTED			
Service Employees International Union Political Ed & Action Fund	22,825,753	25,955,008	Yes
EMILYS List Non Federal	11,776,201	11,128,055	Yes
America Votes, Inc.	9,243,143	9,563,549	No
September Fund	5,230,500	4,950,861	No
America Votes 2006	5,148,750	4,389,203	No
America Coming Together - Nonfederal Account	4,494,107	6,998,238	Yes
Heartland PAC	3,060,177	3,039,146	No
UFCW Active Ballot Club Education Fund	2,235,000	1,927,431	Yes
1199 SEIU NonFederal Committee	2,227,793	2,257,502	Yes
Majority Action	2,157,250	1,995,692	No
Grassroots Democrats	2,039,648	2,584,756	No
Citizens to End Corruption	1,951,830	1,951,840	No
League of Conservation Voters Inc 527	1,923,000	1,512,374	Yes
AFL-CIO COPE - Treasury Fund	1,854,205	1,902,926	Yes
Change to Win Political Education	1,821,072	1,305,406	No
New Democratic Network - Non-Federal Account	1,774,204	1,256,434	Yes
The Lantern Project	1,700,900	1,633,502	No
Young Democrats of America	1,632,929	1,576,603	No
Coloradans For Life	1,375,021	1,524,654	No
The Senate Accountability Project	990,526	987,173	No

527s in 2006 by spending just under $26 million (see Table 3-1). In fact, the five largest 527s of the 2006 cycle were all liberal: SEIU, American Federation of State, County, and Municipal Employees (AFSCME), Progress for America, America Votes, and America Coming Together. Together, these five liberal groups raised an impressive $32 million.[70] This was consistent with the tide of 2006, a heavily Democratic year.

The SEIU spent $2.4 million in the form of independent expenditures on behalf of candidates across the country, all of it either for Democrats ($2 million) or against Republicans ($331,000). Only a negligible $20,000 was spent against Democrats. Of the seventeen Republicans the SEIU spent money opposing, eleven went down to defeat. Of the thirty-four Demo-

Table 3-1 Federal 527 Organizations Raising or Spending $200,000 or More in 2005-06 Cycle

Organization Name	Contributions Received	Expenditures	Associated PAC
REPUBLICAN ORIENTED			
Club For Growth	6,375,280	7,427,414	Yes
Progress for America Voter Fund	6,175,025	12,457,683	No
Economic Freedom Fund	5,050,450	4,835,805	Yes
College Republican National Committee, Inc.	3,720,110	10,260,343	No
Americans For Honesty on Issues	3,030,221	2,830,148	No
National Federation of Republican Women	1,518,658	3,028,197	Yes
Softer Voices	1,403,300	1,266,000	No
Free Enterprise Fund Committee	1,239,003	1,231,630	Yes
American Solutions for Winning Our Future	1,035,000	48,365	No
Americas PAC	959,100	971,747	Yes
Club for Growth.net	841,800	722,720	Yes
The Presidential Coalition, LLC	707,845	7,256,082	Yes
Republicans Who Care Individual Fund	599,300	470,313	No
Black Republican Freedom Fund	416,966	411,642	No
Free Enterprise Committee	400,124	362,822	No
Ohio Effective Government Project	360,000	312,329	No
WISH List Non Federal	350,456	390,471	Yes
Republican National Lawyers	302,070	198,143	No
Stop Her Now	161,337	208,912	No
Citizen Leader Coalition	55,281	523,624	No

cratic races the SEIU became involved in, Democrats won twenty-five.[71]

A good example of SEIU effectiveness was the 2006 Ohio Senate race, a high-profile battle between Republican incumbent Mike DeWine and Democratic representative Sherrod Brown. DeWine's campaign outraised Brown's—$14.2 million to 10.8 million—but the Democrat received much more outside spending than DeWine—a total of $6.5 million versus just $1.6 million for DeWine. The SEIU alone spent $270,000 to elect Brown, who won in November with 56.2 percent of the vote.[72] The outside spending helped Brown reach relative funding parity with DeWine, thus blunting one of the traditional benefits of incumbency.[73]

Another good example of outside group influence was the close

Senate election in Montana, where Democratic state senator John Tester beat three-term Republican senator Conrad Burns by just three thousand votes—one of the two closest and last decided races of the cycle. The Republican incumbent's official campaign outraised his Democratic-challenger's by nearly 2 to 1—$9.4 million to $5.5 million. But liberal outside groups pumped in $3.7 million to Tester's campaign, outspending conservative outside groups by 3 to 1. MoveOn.org donated $62,790 to Tester's campaign, while the SEIU spent $52,500 in ads attacking Burns.[74] In small states like Montana, where media buys are cheap, outside group efforts are even more potent, Tester's victory by the narrowest of margins couldn't have happened without them.

Unions were the story in 2006 for Democrats, across the board. All told, labor unions contributed more than $40 million to pro-Democratic 527s in 2006.

The AFL-CIO spent a total of $40 million on the 2006 elections, focusing its efforts on communicating its election message to its members, numbering in the millions. This was consistent with the AFL-CIO's general practice in election campaigns of focusing most of its resources on voter drives and on-the-ground activities, whereas other unions like SEIU get more involved in spending for and against specific candidates. By contrast, the American Federation of State and Municipal Employees (AFSCME) spent $14.5 million, $2 million of it in federal elections, of which 98 percent was spent on Democrats' behalf. Another $4.5 million was spent on independent expenditures concerning specific candidates—most of it targeting Republicans.

AFSCME also organized, with other labor groups, the 527 Americans United For Change, which placed ads in twenty-five targeted "most critical House and Senate races." Nancy Pelosi and Harry Reid met with potential donors for the group, and the AFSCME helped fund it.[75]

One of the biggest themes of the 2006 races was the Republican corruption scandals in the wake of the Jack Abramoff affair. Americans United For Change ran ads around election time highlighting current examples of corruption—"Republican leaders are indicted for money laundering"—and urging support of the Honest Leadership Act, a lobbying and ethics reform bill put out by congressional Democratic leaders. As a CFI report noted: "The advertisement contained neither an explicit electoral message nor mentioned a candidate but in context—given the timing and placement of the ads—could be seen as implicitly supporting a partisan electoral change."[76] Americans United for Change also aired an ad in Pennsylvania warning of cuts in Social Security. In context, it was clearly aimed at Senator Rick Santorum, who would go on to lose his seat by a whopping 18 points. But it was also more broadly framed to tap into Americans' misgivings about President Bush's unsuccessful attempt to privatize Social Security.

MoveOn.org also hit House Republicans with the GOP corruption theme, while tapping into voter discontent with the war in Iraq. MoveOn spent $444,424 against twelve-term Republican congresswoman Nancy Johnson of Connecticut. Johnson outraised her Democratic challenger, Christopher Murphy, but MoveOn and other outside groups helped Murphy blunt this advantage.[77] He won the seat. MoveOn's help was also crucial in Pennsylvania's Fourth Congressional District, where three-term Republican incumbent Melissa Hart was considered invulnerable. But MoveOn provided $448,000 to the upstart campaign of Democrat Jason Altmire, who beat Hart in a close race.[78]

Another major 527 player was the September Fund, established by former Clinton administration deputy chief of staff Harold Ickes. Aside from spending on its own advertisements, the September Fund also gave to other outside groups. It spent nearly $5 million in the 2006 campaign, despite its late start (as suggested by its name).

The September Fund offers a textbook example of how 527s make a mockery of federal requirements. As the law stipulates, 527s cannot "coordinate" with specific candidates or with party committees—yet Ickes was a classic insider, with ties to most important Democrats. As with other big 527 players in 2006, the September Fund's leadership was closely tied to organized labor: its leadership included Karen Ackerman, the political director of the AFL-CIO, and Anna Burger, chairwoman of the Change to Win labor federation.

One of the left's important mechanisms to coordinate all of this activity in 2006 was ActBlue, a political committee founded in 2004 that soon became an online "clearinghouse" for Democratic candidates, both state and federal. The Web-based PAC was established in 2004 by two young technology geeks who had met at an MIT summer program, but it didn't really hit its stride until the 2006 election cycle. The ActBlue website allows individuals to channel the money of friends, family, and like-minded voters into a significant donation for their favorite candidates. Users could navigate the ActBlue website to view virtually every Democratic candidate and ballot initiative across the country and donate online if they wished. Individuals could become fundraisers for their favorite candidates or give to candidates at the suggestion of others.

ActBlue worked effectively as a centralized hub for Democratic giving in 2006, raising just under $16 million.[79] Since its inception, it has distributed nearly $200 million to Democratic candidates of all "ideological persuasions," ranging from Barack Obama's presidential bid to small state and local races. Of this, only about $55 million has been reported, not because of any illegal contributions but "because much of that money comes in donations below the $200 threshold for itemized disclosure."[80]

INDIVIDUAL PLAYERS

The steadiest trend of this decade in campaign finance—the increasingly exclusive role of super-wealthy donors or politically connected interest groups—continued in 2006. "The main funding source for federal 527s is large individual donations, followed by labor union contributions," the Campaign Finance Institute reported of the 2006 campaign.[81] Nearly half of all 527 contributions came from donors giving $100,000 or more, three times as much as these donors had provided in 2002.[82]

The fifty largest individual donors to federal 527s in 2006, in fact, contributed $42 million—the same amount as the unions (Table 3-2).

Texas homebuilder Bob Perry donated $8.15 million and media mogul Jerry Perenchio gave $6 million to pro-Republican 527s. Perry's donations were parceled out among three 527 groups supporting at least fifteen GOP candidates with media advertising. On the Democratic side, financier George Soros gave $3.89 million and hotel heiress and investor Linda Pritzker gave $2.43 million.[83]

Though Soros didn't hover over Democratic efforts in the same imposing way he had in 2004, his presence was still profoundly influen-

Table 3-2 2006 Individual 527 Donors of $100,000 or More and Their Contributions to Federal Political Committees

527 Donor	527 Total	Total Federal	Congressional	PAC	Party
Bob J. Perry	$9,750,000	$91,800	$32,600	$20,000	$35,000
Jerry Perenchino	6,000,000	39,900	27,000	9,400	3,500
Geroge Soros	3,890,000	95,382	34,450		60,932
Linda Prtizker	2,381,000	68,000	30,000	2,000	36,000
Peter B. Lewis	1,724,375	9,200	4,200	5,000	
John Hunting	1,370,000	80,650	38,150	10,000	32,500
Dr. John M. Templeton	1,161,515	135,450	30,050	8,000	97,400
Lewis Cullman	1,087,000	119,000	47,000	12,000	60,000
Pat Stryker	1,026,313	45,400	10,400		35,000
Sheldon G. Adelson	1,000,000	103,500	23,400	25,000	56,100
Alida Messinger	928,000	120,300	39,800	30,500	50,000
Virginia Manheimer	861,090	50,000	35,000	15,000	
Carl Lindner Jr.	801,321	99,800	32,300	10,000	52,500
John Harris	773,000	35,000		35,000	
Richard Gilder	600,000	41,650	31,650	10,000	
Arthur Lipson	598,000	103,700	27,300	23,000	53,400
Tim Gill	575,395	98,300	27,300	15,000	56,000
Frank Brunckhorst	575,000	74,950	19,700	20,250	35,000
Jackson Stephens, Jr.	575,000	56,100	46,100	10,000	
Anne G. Earhart	535,000	96,700	34,300	11,000	51,400

tial. During the 2006 election campaign, he contributed only $95,382 in limited "hard money" to federal candidates and party committees, saving most of his donations for independent expenditures. The bulk of his 527 spending went to America Votes, which the CFI describes as "a hybrid associated with both independent groups and party-related figures."

The list of names and groups associated with America Votes reads like a who's who of the progressive left: its organizers included EMILY's List founder Ellen Malcolm, former Sierra Club executive Carl Pope, Harold Ickes, and former SEIU president Andy Stern. Its member organizations included the AFL-CIO, AFSCME, the International Brotherhood of Teamsters, SEIU, and the NAACP National Voter Fund.

Soros was also the largest investor in another company Ickes created, Catalist, which built databases of politically active voters and made them available to Democratic interest groups. Catalist would play an even larger role in 2008.

●●●●●●●●●

501(C) GROUPS

In addition to 527s, the 2006 cycle also saw increased activity from non-profit 501(c)3 advocacy groups, some of which had been created in response to recent Federal Election Commission regulatory moves that had restricted or even ended some 527s' ability to raise political money.

The great advantage these groups possess is that their finances are mostly undisclosed to the public, so they can operate under less scrutiny than 527 groups. So just as 527s themselves arose out of gaps—the "527 loophole"—in the McCain-Feingold law, so 501(c) groups evolved in response to new FEC regulations of 527s. The world of campaign finance remained endlessly adaptive. The 501(c) groups—broken out into (c)(4) social-welfare groups, (c)(5) trade union, and (c)(6) business leagues—would play a bigger role in 2008.

Among the beneficiaries of the 527 loophole was organized labor. FEC regulations primarily affect 527s, but many labor unions found that they could raise money for political candidates through creating 501(c)s instead.[84] This allowed such groups to make unlimited, unregulated soft-money donations for essentially the same purposes as 527s. For a 501(c), the FEC only requires that "political campaign intervention" or "federal campaign activity" not be the "primary activity" or "major purpose" of the organization. This lack of restrictions on 501(c)s has made it easier for some labor organizations to affect elections through campaign financing.

Ultimately, however, conservative-affiliated groups took the lead in this kind of organization. Some of the main players included the American Taxpayers Alliance, Americans for Job Security, the Chamber of Commerce, Common Sense of Ohio, Focus on the Family Action, FreedomWorks, the National Rifle Association, and the National Right to Life Committee.[85]

The nondisclosure makes some of this guesswork, but it seems that the National Rifle Association may have been near the top in terms of (c)(4) giving in 2006. The NRA's campaign war chest was reportedly $20 million, of which about $9 million was routed through its nonprofit arm. The NRA tends to spend money in election years on voter identification, registration, and mobilization. It confirmed to the CFI that most of its activities in 2006 were on behalf of Republicans.[86]

THE 2008 ELECTIONS: OUTSIDE GROUPS AND THE OBAMA TIDAL WAVE

In 2008, some of the 2006 patterns remained, while new trends appeared, as well. But the most important trend was this: money talked. From the presidential race—where Barack Obama built a nearly 2-to-1 financial advantage over John McCain—to congressional races, the candidate with the most money prevailed in the overwhelming number of races.

The most important single development in 2008 was Obama's unprecedented fundraising prowess, which culminated in his decision to opt out of the public financing system for the general election. He became the first major-party presidential candidate to do so since the system was instituted in 1976.[87] And he pointed the way to a future in which campaigns will become fundamentally defined by a race for cash: in 2012, both Obama and Mitt Romney opted out of the public financing system, the first time both candidates have done so. It marks, for all intents and purposes, the end of the public financing system.

It's important, too, to dispel one of the myths of the 2008 Obama campaign—and I'm not talking about "hope" and "change." I'm talking about money. Obama's supporters (understandably) have taken pride in his fundraising ability and often touted his skillful campaign to reach millions of small donors. His success at doing so, they've argued, demonstrates the democratic merits of his candidacy, setting him apart from many typical candidates (of both parties) who draw most of their political money from the usual suspects—big donors and party committees.

The truth, however, is different: in fact, Obama raised about the same percentage of his funding from small donors as George W. Bush did in 2004. In fact, Obama got about 80 percent more money from his large donors (cumulative contributions of at least $1,000) than from his small donors.[88] This doesn't negate the impressive innovations his campaign developed—like online social networking—or the appeal of his candidacy in 2008, but it offers some needed perspective.

At the end of the day in our current system, a candidate who can't raise big money from the big donors isn't going to be in the game for very long. And this is the core problem with the entire system and why it poses a threat to our democracy.

Even with his enormous fundraising clout, Obama's candidacy inspired plenty of outside-group spending in 2008 on his behalf. But overall, the impact of these groups on the Democratic side was felt most strongly in House and Senate elections, where such funding was arguably much more necessary.

The higher-spending candidate won 93 percent of House of Representatives races and 94 percent of Senate races, according to a post-election analysis by the nonpartisan Center for Responsive Politics. In the Senate that figure represented a huge spike up from 2006, when the higher-spending Senate candidate won 73 percent of the races. The average cost of winning a House race in 2008 was nearly $1.1 million and almost $6.5 million for a Senate seat.[89]

As the Campaign Finance Institute summarized: "In an unusual election where the Democratic presidential candidate raised astounding amounts of money, both major candidates discouraged soft-money support, and the gathering recession discouraged some prospective wealthy individual donors, outside soft money still made a big impression—particularly in close Senate and House races."[90]

● ● ● ● ● ● ●

UNION POWER

In 2008, labor organizations continued to impact elections through campaign financing—led once again by the SEIU, the year's top 527, which spent $85 million during the course of the election cycle.[91] Even though Obama's campaign was already the best funded in history, the SEIU spent a staggering $27.7 million on it.[92] But the union didn't confine its energies to the White House. The chart below shows the top recipients of funds from SEIU for the 2008 election cycle, and whether or not those candidates succeeded in their campaigns for public office.[93]

Of the twenty candidates that SEIU donated to, fourteen won. SEIU gave

Table 3-3. Election Outcomes of Candidates Receiving Donations

Recipient	Election Outcome	Amount
Barack Obama (President)	Won	$74, 578
Donald Cazayoux (Senate)	Lost	$22,500
Bill Foster (HOR)	Won	$20,000
Al Franken (Senate)	Won	$20,000
Donna Edwards (HOR)	Won	$18,500
Laura Richardson* (HOR)	Won	$17,500
Mary Jo Kilroy (HOR)	Won	$15,000
James Francis Martin (Senate)	Lost	$15,000
Harry Teague (HOR)	Won	$15,000
Jay Rockefeller* (Senate)	Won	$12,300
Judith Feder (HOR)	Lost	$11,250
Joe Garcia (HOR)	Lost	$11,000
John Edwards (Presidential primary)	Lost	$10,800
Eric Massa (HOR)	Won	$10,750
Nancy Pelosi* (HOR)	Won	$10,650
George Miller* (HOR)	Won	$10,600
Jan Schakowsky* (HOR)	Won	$10,600
Ashwin Madia (HOR)	Lost	$10,500
Dina Titus (HOR)	Won	$10,500
Mark Begich (Senate)	Won	$10,250
*Incumbent.		

$12,000 or more to ten candidates, nine of which won their elections. The success rate is even more impressive considering that the majority of these candidates were challengers, not incumbents—and incumbents typically come to political campaigns with more money and donors than non-incumbents.

Following in SEIU's wake, the American Federation of State, County and Municipal Employees spent $63 million,[94] the International Brotherhood of Teamsters spent $13 million,[95] and the United Auto Workers spent $11 million.[96] This money was used in a variety of ways to support the Obama campaign and advocate against the McCain campaign and Republicans generally. AFSCME also donated $3.15 million in October 2008 alone, to Patriot

Majority, which ran ads against Senators Elizabeth Dole, Roger Wicker, and Saxby Chambliss.[97]

Simply put, unions were responsible for an enormous amount of pro-Obama campaign efforts during the election cycle.

● ● ● ● ● ● ●

527S AND 501S

More broadly, the Democrats continued their edge among 527 groups, while the Republican advantage among 501(c) groups counterbalanced it almost dollar for dollar.

Among 527s, Democratic-leaning groups spent $143 million to Republican-oriented groups' $56 million. Among 501(c)s, meanwhile, the story was almost the mirror image: Republican-leaning groups spent $142 million to Democratic-supporting groups' $54 million.[98]

Consistent with past trends, seven of the top ten largest 527s in 2008 were liberal. The biggest group once again was SEIU, followed by AFSCME, the National Association of Realtors, MoveOn.org, and the United Auto Workers. All told, the two different kinds of soft-money groups spent over $400 million on the 2008 election campaign, about split halfway between them. For the 527s, the approximately $200 million represented a huge drop from the peak year of 2004, when 527 groups spent $400 million themselves. The main reason for the drop-off was not only various regulatory changes at the FEC, but Obama's staggering success in raising money independently for his presidential campaign.

Yet outside groups still played a major role in 2008, and the drop-off in 527 funding was more than compensated for by the large spike in donations to 501(c) groups. These groups' prominence is all the more impressive, moreover, given that both Obama and Senator John McCain discouraged giving to outside groups, casting themselves as reformers. Both candidates discouraged giving to these groups, but they flourished nonetheless, demonstrating their political autonomy—and their continued ability to make an impact on elections.

With the presidential election awash in money, 501(c) groups directed substantial portions of their funding toward issue campaigns. Many conservative-oriented groups rallied against the potential passage of the Employee Free Choice Act, also known as "card check"—a bill that would make it much easier to start unions in workplaces by allowing employees simply to check off a card indicating their willingness to join. The Coalition for a Democratic Workplace, made up of business groups opposed to the legislation, put money into TV ads directed at swing voters and warning them of the dangers of the legislation. "Our strategy is simple," said Richard Berman, the head of another anti-card-check group, Employee Freedom Action Committee. "I'm trying to make this a defining issue for voters in their particular races."[99]

The most formidable counterpart to the SEIU on the right, among the 501(c) groups, was the Chamber of Commerce. The Chamber, a self-declared nonpartisan group, set out to prevent the Democrats from attaining a supermajority in the Senate—sixty seats. The Chamber's 501(c) organization targeted five key Senate races, spending a third of their total $35 million outlay on efforts to reelect five GOP senators: Norm Coleman in Minnesota, Mitch McConnell in Kentucky, Elizabeth Dole in North Carolina, Roger Wicker in Mississippi, and John Sununu in New Hampshire. Republicans won just two—McConnell and Wicker—but those two were just enough to prevent the feared Democratic supermajority. The Democrats picked up eight seats, taking a 59–41 majority. [100]

Typical of the Chamber's ads during the cycle—and according to CFI, representative in general of the characteristics of 501(c) advertising—was its TV ad against Coleman's opponent in Minnesota, Al Franken. Making reference to Franken's former career as a comedian, the ad opened with show business music and a photo of Franken with duct tape over his mouth. As the tape is removed to reveal a crooked smile, a voiceover says: "High taxes hurt. But it seems like every time Al Franken opens his mouth he talks about raising taxes. This from a guy who was caught not paying his own taxes in seventeen states." The ad concludes by urging viewers: "Tell Al Franken that high taxes aren't very funny." As with most such 501(c) efforts, the Franken ad connected a candidate to a specific issue (in this case high taxes), and urged viewers, vaguely, to let the candidate know how they feel about the issue—without ever urging them explicitly to vote against him.

The Franken-Coleman race was notable for other reasons: it was the last decided race of the season, not being legally declared over for six months; and, decided by just 300 votes, it was a race in which outside money played an important role. Liberal groups pumped nearly $1.6 million into the state to support Franken, but conservative groups spent barely half that to support Coleman. This outside-group advantage was particularly important to Franken given that, as in so many other races, the two official campaigns were on roughly equal financial footing: about $21 million each. In an election decided by 0.01 percent of the vote, every dollar proved to be critical.

Outside-group spending was crucial in taking another Republican

Senate seat in New Hampshire, this one held by John Sununu. Liberal groups spent nearly $1 million supporting Democratic candidate Jeanne Shaheen and over $1.8 million on attack ads against Sununu; by contrast, conservative groups mustered less than $200,000 in Sununu's defense and spent not a penny attacking Shaheen, who went on to win, 51 percent to 45 percent. Once again, the two candidates' official campaigns raised and spent nearly equal amounts of money; the outside-group funding advantage proved crucial for Shaheen.

CATALIST

As in 2008, the issues favored Democrats, if not as dramatically. They had a unique presidential candidate and enormously motivated grassroots groups, union participation, NAACP voter drives, and robust 527 support. But what few know about is another tool that may have played a significant role in the party's big win—and which is linked, inextricably, to the new world of campaign finance. That tool was a supercharged database of likely voters, funded and made possible in significant part by George Soros.

The database, called Catalist, was created by Harold Ickes. Ickes spent $15 million building the database, which scored 230 million Americans according to their voting proclivities. Ickes modeled the database on VoterVault, a similar effort that gave Republicans a big edge in voter targeting in both 2000 and 2004. "We have lost," Ickes said, "because we did not have the technical capability of finding voters that we needed to find and get them out to vote." Using Catalist, the Obama campaign generated detailed data on swing voters, including specifics like which ones "would be receptive to a pitch based on Obama's 'change' theme, and which may be more interested in his health-care or energy policies."[101]

The Obama campaign wasn't the only progressive organization using Catalist, though. Some eighty progressive groups—from the League of Conservation Voters to Planned Parenthood—purchase data from the company, and other candidates, like former Virginia governor Mark Warner, used the database in his campaign for the Senate. So did the Democratic Congressional and Senate committees and a range of 527 groups. How successful was it? *The Atlantic's* Marc Ambinder put it in perspective:

According to the analysis, those registered voters contacted by Catalist member groups turned out at a rate of 74.6 percent; the voters who weren't turned out in proportions roughly equivalent to the national average—about 60.4 percent. In four states, the number of new votes cast by liberals exceeded Obama's victory margin: in Ohio, Florida, Indiana and North Carolina. If you assume that only 60 percent of these voters chose Obama, the margin was still greater than Obama's in North Carolina and Indiana, both essential to his victory. With the caveat that correlation does not equal causation, the report provides convincing, if not absolute, evidence that the progressive/Democratic data-mining and targeting operation measurably helped elect Barack Obama.[102]{/EXT}

With results like that for Democrats, it shouldn't be surprising that George Soros had a hand in it somewhere. Though his prominence in 2006 and 2008 didn't match the high profile he enjoyed in 2004, he remained an important player behind the scenes and a continuing source of vital funding. And more symbolically, he remains representative of one of the

dominant facts about outside-spending groups: without the role of super
elites (from unions to corporations to business groups) and the super
wealthy (like Soros), these groups couldn't operate.

CONCLUSION

The 2006 and 2008 elections represented milestones in the participation of outside groups in the political process. Both years saw records set for spending—either by midterm or presidential-election standards—and both years revealed how adaptive both 527 and 501(c) groups, and their organizers and supporters, remained in the wake of both McCain-Feingold and the continuing (if futile) efforts of the FEC to establish some semblance of transparency and some limit to political influence. Both years were also big ones for Democrats—a recapture of both houses of Congress in 2006 and a retaking of the White House in 2008.

The elections showed the potency of an aroused Democratic base—especially organized labor—and its ability to raise and spend political money to shape electoral outcomes. SEIU's outlay was so ambitious, in fact, that it prompted fears that the union had overextended itself financially. But from the union's perspective, the spending had practical benefits beyond Obama's election: the new president named several officials with SEIU backgrounds to sensitive administration posts. And the administration took on the union's two highest priorities: health-care reform and card check (winning one, losing the other).[103]

After wins like 2006 and 2008, the Democrats in a sense had nowhere to go but down, and the Republicans nowhere but up—and in 2010, this is precisely what would happen.

Helping lead the charge to bring the Republicans back to some measure of political power in Washington were reinvigorated conservative independent-expenditure groups. In part, this new energy was an inevitable result of being a minority party in the opposition: conservative groups were faced with a Democratic president and Democratic majorities in both houses of Congress, so they had plenty of motivation going into the 2010 midterm elections.

But in January of 2010 the Supreme Court would hand down a ruling that fundamentally transformed the campaign finance landscape—and for 2010, at least, that transformation would work decisively in the GOP's favor.

4

The First *Citizens United* Election: 2010

There is clear reason for ordinary citizens to be concerned that this divisive ruling will, in reality, allow powerful corporations to drown out the voices of everyday Americans in future campaigns. This ruling is no doubt yet another victory for Wall Street, at the expense of Main Street America.

Senator Patrick Leahy (D-VT), January 21, 2010,

on the Supreme Court's ruling in Citizens United[104]

What the Supreme Court did is a combination of arrogance, naivete and stupidity the likes of which I have never seen.

Senator John McCain (R-AZ), March 28, 2012[105]

Citizens United and its follow-on rulings—*Speechnow.org v. FEC* and the ruling by U.S. district judge James Cacheris striking down the long-standing ban on direct corporate contributions to federal candidates—opened up the floodgates to a new universe of campaign finance. How transformative these rulings would be was made clear right away, in the first elections to take place under the new system—the 2010 midterms. The elections were flooded with money from independent-expenditure groups, both super PACs and nonprofits. Often, but not always, they achieved desired outcomes.

The 2010 midterm elections produced three outcomes of crucial consequence.

First, the Republican Party retook the House of Representatives, a result not possible—as I will show—without the leading financial role of independent-expenditure groups.

Second, the political and financial influence of these groups pushed the Republican Party further rightward—an influence that ultimately shaped both victories (a conservative House majority) and defeats (a lost chance to regain the Senate from the Democrats). The power of outside groups was made clear not just in general-election races but in the primaries—most dramatically, in the Senate primary defeats of Republican front-runners in Delaware, Colorado, Kentucky, Nevada, and Florida. In these states, ultra-conservative Republican candidates enjoying crucial financial support of outside groups wrested the party's nomination from more moderate candidates. In three of those five states, however, the GOP candidate went down to defeat in November—dooming the party's chances of recapturing the Senate but ratifying the power of outside, independent groups in our political process. This push, a direct result of the power these groups now wield, has irrevocably changed the Republican Party. Consider, for instance, the blatant attempts of longtime Republican senators Richard Lugar and Orrin Hatch to curry favor with the hard-core right wing in order to hold onto their seats—unsuccessfully, in Lugar's case. These efforts will only increase in number and intensity in the future, as the flow of money shows no signs of slowing down.

Third, the 2010 elections, while mostly a disaster for the Democratic Party, were not a disaster for is most tenacious constituency: labor unions. This is because the unions further consolidated their hold on Democratic Party politics and policy—and they did so as a direct result of the *Citizens United* and *SpeechNow* decisions. Unions no longer need to rely solely on dues to finance attack ads, and thus have more money free to contribute directly to candidates. The three largest unions—AFSCME, AFL-CIO, and the NEA—spent upwards of $172 million, $30 million more than the Chamber of Commerce, a reliable conservative player. AFSCME, in fact, is estimated to have spent a total of $91 million, nearly one-third of all pro-Democratic independent spending.[106] The result of all this is, of course, a Democratic Party largely beholden to unions—which means a party more ideologically left and less likely to find middle ground with the opposition. Though 2010 wasn't a Democratic year, Democratic leaders know where to go for campaign funding—and the unions, like their conservative super-PAC counterparts, will hold considerable leverage over their policy positions.

With the outsized importance super PACs now have on our politics, it can be easy to forget that they are a phenomenon barely two years old. The first super PACs began appearing in July 2010. Though they were required to report their donors, either monthly or quarterly, to the FEC, and were prohibited from donating money directly to political candidates, the new groups operated within a much freer landscape than previously. They could raise unlimited sums of money from corporations, unions, associations and individuals, and then spend unlimited sums to advocate overtly for or against political candidates. Even observers who decried the court rulings in early 2010 had to be astonished at how quickly, and expertly, political power brokers refashioned fundraising structures to their own advantage.

●●●●●●●

THE BIG PLAYERS IN 2010

For those who doubted whether *Citizens United* and *Speechnow.org* would open up the financial floodgates, consider: 2010 super PAC financial disclosure reports showed that "much of their funding [came] from private-equity partners and others in the financial industry."[107] Much of the private-equity money went toward opposing Democrats: John Childs, founder of Boston-based J. W. Childs Associates, gave $650,000 to the Club for Growth, an anti-tax group closely affiliated with the GOP, while Dalea Partners, a private-equity firm based in Oklahoma City, gave $250,000 to the First Amendment Alliance, which spent money opposing five Democratic Senate candidates, including Harry Reid and Michael Bennet.

In all, eighty-four super PACs organized during the 2010 election cycle and reported total receipts of $84.9 million, of which they spent $65.3 million. That might sound somewhat modest by today's standards—just $1 million raised per super PAC—but the breakdown is extremely skewed. In reality, a much smaller group of sixteen super PACs dominated the fundraising and were the only ones to raise $1 million or more. As Table

Table 4-1. The Sweet Sixteen: Super PACs That Raised More Than $1 Million During the 2010 Midterm Elections

Group	Independent Expenditures	Viewpoint	Total Raised
American Crossroads	$21,553,277	Conservative	$26,575,589
America's Families First Action Fund	$ 5,878,743	Liberal	$ 7,083,010
Club for Growth Action	$ 4,996,980	Conservative	$ 5,589,334
NEA Advocacy Fund	$ 4,200,000	Liberal	$ 3,300,000
Women Vote!	$ 3,628,645	Liberal	$ 6,505,040
Commonsense Ten	$ 3,257,033	Liberal	$ 4,263,304
Our Future Ohio PAC	$ 3,068,144	Liberal	$ 3,216,000
Patriot Majority	$ 1,968,700	Liberal	$ 3,389,335
Super PAC for America	$ 1,633,786	Conservative	$ 4,467,933
First Amendment Alliance	$ 1,487,861	Conservative	$ 1,816,883
New Prosperity Foundation	$ 1,478,923	Conservative	$ 1,822,095
Alaskans Standing Together	$ 1,260,000	Conservative	$ 1,824,000
Ending Spending Fund	$ 1,150,000	Conservative	$ 1,180,672
Natl Assn of Realtors Congressional Fund	$ 1,097,266		$ 1,105,625
Majority Action	$ 986,607	Liberal	$ 1,094,320

4-1 shows, those sixteen super PACs alone raised over $74 million.

Briefly, let's take a closer look at the three top-spending groups in this list—two conservative and one liberal.

AMERICAN CROSSROADS

It's almost unfair to compare any other independent group, at least in 2010, to American Crossroads, a super PAC that spent nearly four times as much as the second-place spender, the liberal America's Families First Action Fund. Founded by a group of Republican political players affiliated with the George W. Bush administration—including senior presidential adviser Karl Rove—American Crossroads brought in an astonishing $26.5 million and spent $21.5 million of it on independent expenditures.[108] Crossroads' website mission statement includes a call for Americans to choose sides on the political battlefront: "We face a decision between two starkly different visions of America: one where the human creativity and initiative that are unleashed by liberty and free enterprise generate the economic growth this nation needs—and one where an increasingly powerful, all-controlling federal government decides how to allocate the economic spoils."[109]

While that appeal refrains from identifying with a specific party, the fact remains that in 2010, nearly all of Crossroads' expenditures were put toward rhetoric against Democrats. Of the $21.5 million it spent on the 2010 election, $17 million went to funding anti-Democratic advertisements.[110] And although Crossroads claims that it is an "independent expenditure-only committee,"[111] in the 2010 election cycle, it donated $1.2 million to the Republican State Leadership Committee, which gives direct financial support to state and local Republican candidates.[112]

American Crossroads' influential founders, huge financial backing, and goals for defeating Democrats through excessive spending embody the group's status as perhaps the definitive super PAC. Along with Rove, the former chairman of the Republican National Committee, Ed Gillespie, was instrumental in its founding, though neither serves officially on its board. In its first financial quarter of existence, the group raised $4.2 million and on a few occasions spent half a million dollars on independent expenditures in a single week—actions that had been illegal just months earlier.[113]

Unlike most other PACs, American Crossroads did not get its funding by bundling together small donations. Instead, of the $4.2 million it raised in that first quarter, 97 percent came from just *four* donors. Trevor Rees-Jones, president of Dallas-based Chief Oil and Gas, gave $1 million. Bradley Wayne Hughes, chairman of Public Storage Inc., was American Crossroads' biggest donor for a time, contributing $1.55 million. A company called Southwest Louisiana Land LLC (Harold Simmons, about whom more later, is board chairman) donated $1 million.[114] And TRT Holdings, owned by Dallas's Robert Rowling, gave American Crossroads $1 million. (Three of these four donors are based in Texas.).[115]

In fact, 98.6 percent of American Crossroads' total money raised in the 2010 election cycle came from donations of greater than $200 (an average donation of $32,648 from 814 individuals). The group's single biggest donor in 2010 was Texas homebuilder Bob Perry, who donated $7 million to the group between September 1 and October 13.[116] Perry has a history of financial support for conservative political causes; he was the major funder of Swift Boat Veterans for Truth, the group that did so much to damage the presidential campaign of John Kerry in 2004.

Crossroads received "six- and seven-figure donations from the financial industry," including "$500,000 from Anne Dias-Griffin, founder of the Aragon Global Management hedge fund, and her husband, Kenneth Griffin, founder of the Citadel Investment Group hedge fund." Power brokers like the Griffins are putting down a financial stake to ensure certain policies— such as staving off Democratic efforts to levy taxes on carried interest, an issue that has resurfaced.

AMERICA'S FAMILIES FIRST ACTION FUND

The second-highest spending super PAC of 2010 was this liberal group devoted to preserving the Democratic majority in the House, which it chose to pursue by focusing on several competitive House races in which large cash influxes could have dramatic effects. By doing so, it hoped to create a "firewall" that would deny the Republicans the House. The Fund worked with other already existing independent liberal groups to meet the needs of Democratic candidates in these races. One strategy the Fund employed was to paint Republicans in key races as extremists.

According to the *New York Times*, which obtained a document from the group outlining their strategy, the top team of political operatives running the group included: Peter Cari, a former political director of the Democratic Congressional Campaign Committee; Will Robinson, a former campaign director for the Democratic National Committee; Cristina Uribe, who served as the western regional director for EMILY's List; and Frank Smith, a lawyer who has worked with independent groups. The executive director of another liberal group, America Votes, Greg Speeds, also worked with America's Families First Action Fund to help provide important field information on specific races. Major donors to the group included prominent labor and environmental groups.[117]

CLUB FOR GROWTH

Club for Growth, a not-for-profit organized in 1999 that advocates for conservative economic policies, offers a prime example of how special-interest money is driving politics to extremes. The Club is devoted to a hard-core, free-market message of low taxation and business-friendly policies. The Club's website notes: "At the beginning of the 20th century, federal taxes accounted for 3 percent of the nation's gross domestic product, and federal tax rules filled just a few hundred pages. Today, federal taxes account for more than 18 percent of GDP, and federal tax rules and regulations span over 60,000 pages."[118] The group champions a number of other conservative policies, including spending cuts, "federal death-tax repeal," expanding trade freedoms, privatizing Social Security, reforming the medical malpractice and tort system, deregulation, and increased educational choices.[119]

What makes the Club unique is its willingness to play hardball even against nominally friendly Republicans whom it deems too moderate. It has bankrolled right-wing primary challengers to centrist Republican officeholders or party-backed candidates. The Club's ideological passion doesn't always lead to positive results. That became clear in 2009, when it backed the Conservative Party's Doug Hoffman over mainstream Republican Party nominee Deirdre Scozzafava in the special election in New York's Twenty-third Congressional District. Scozzafava eventually pulled out of the election and threw her support to the Democrat, Bill Owens, who beat Hoffman narrowly on Election Day.

In 2010, the Club spent $2.5 million, qualifying for the "Heavy Hitter" designation from Open Secrets.[120] It spent lavishly on TV ads to oust respected Republican senator Bob Bennett of Utah, whom it pilloried for voting for TARP and other federal spending. Bennett was ousted at his party's convention in the spring, where he finished third on the ballot. As Club president Chris Chocola (a former congressman) wrote in an email, the defeat of Bennett marked "the *first time* the Club's PAC has defeated an incumbent Republican senator. It will set off a political earthquake in Congress."[121] And it did: Bennett's Senate seat was won by Tea Party supporter Mike Lee, who enjoyed support from the Club in his fall campaign.[122]

Lee's victory was just one dramatic result among many in what should be remembered as the first super PAC election.

●●●●●●●●

2010: THE FIRST SUPER PAC ELECTION

For Republicans, 2010 was a big year: the party regained control of the House of Representatives and came close to doing the same in the Senate. So it shouldn't be surprising to see that GOP-oriented super PACs led the way in spending. Refer back to Table 4-1 showing the top sixteen super PACs: while eight were identified as liberal, seven conservative, and one somewhere in the middle, the seven conservative super PACs substantially outraised the eight liberal super PACs, 58 percent to 40 percent. In fact, the seven conservative super PACs raised *more than half of all the money* raised by super PACs in the 2010 midterm elections.

Where did the money go? In the broadest sense, it was well distributed across both Senate and House races. As we will see, super PACs were decisive in winning back the House for the GOP. They were also decisive—this time in a negative sense—in the GOP's failure to recapture the Senate. Both results are indicative of the stranglehold independent-expenditure groups now have on party politics.

American Crossroads focused heavily on a select group of Senate races as the GOP made a serious run at retaking the chamber. In particular, it focused its fiscal cannons on about a dozen key Democratic Senate candidates, both incumbents and challengers: Senate Majority Leader Harry Reid (D-NV), Senator Michael Bennet (D-CO), Senator Patty Murray (D-WA), Senator Barbara Boxer (D-CA), Senator Blanche Lincoln (D-AR), and Senator Russ Feingold (D-WI). Among challengers, it targeted Jack Conway in Kentucky, Alexi Giannoulias in Illinois, Joe Manchin in West Virginia, Robin Carnahan in Missouri, Lee Fisher in Ohio, Paul Hodes in New Hampshire, and Joe Sestak in Pennsylvania.[123]

Eight of the ten races American Crossroads spent the most on were Senate races—led by the $5 million it spent attempting (unsuccessfully) to defeat Bennet in Colorado. In those eight Senate races, the Crossroads-supported candidate prevailed in five. These included the $2.3 million it spent to defeat Robin Carnahan in Missouri, the $1.4 million it spent against Jack Conway, who lost to Rand Paul in Kentucky, and the $1.1 million it spent to help Mark Kirk beat Alex Giannoulias in Illinois.

Crossroads spent lavishly in Ohio to win the open Senate seat for Rob Portman, a former Bush administration official. Portman won easily. The Colorado senate race was one of the nation's most expensive, with over $30 million being spent by outside groups. Incumbent senator Bennet was the number one target of super PAC groups—they spent $6.9 million against him—yet he somehow survived by a single percentage point over Republican Ken Buck.[124] Senate Majority Leader Harry Reid—target number two, with about $3 million spent against him—also held on to his seat.[125]

In Reid's case, he was likely saved by the GOP's nomination of an extremely marginal and flawed opponent: Sharron Angle. The Club for Growth was the key super PAC behind the extreme-right-wing, Tea Party–supported Angle, endorsing her with three weeks left in her primary battle against Sue Lowden. In the primary campaign's remaining three weeks, the Club spent $238,455 in ads targeting Lowden. To put this in perspective, this is nearly $18,000 more than they spent on ads against Senator Reid, $50,000 more than they spent against Senator Feingold, and a host of other Senate and House races.[126] Angle also got vital financial support from the Tea Party Express.

Sue Lowden was no liberal Republican: she garnered endorsements from conservative stalwarts like Rush Limbaugh and Sean Hannity, the NRA, the Susan B. Anthony List, Senator Jon Kyl, former senator Fred Thompson and his wife, Jeri Thompson, and former Nevada governor Robert List. But she ran one of Politico's "Worst Campaigns of 2010," stumbling with her suggestion that people could barter to reduce health-care costs, and then continued with a controversy over the use of a supporter's RV and poor handling of a question regarding the Voting Rights Act.[127]

Angle won the nomination, but she was trounced by Reid in November. Lowden had been projected to beat Reid.

More successfully, the Club for Growth also supported Marco Rubio, who won the Florida senate seat. Rubio's status as a favorite of outside independent groups became clear in the spring, when he won the GOP nomination after former governor Charlie Crist—who had once been seen as the shoe-in nominee—saw the writing on the wall and pulled out of the race, declaring himself an independent. Rubio then beat Crist and Democrat Kendrick Meek in the November general election.

The Club for Growth also supported Pat Toomey—who had served as the Club's president—in his successful run for the Senate in Pennsylvania. Toomey had been a perennial challenger to longtime centrist GOP senator Arlen Specter. As Rubio had done with Crist, Toomey eventually drove Specter out of the Republican Party (and out of his Senate seat). But the Club also backed ultra-conservative Ken Buck in his losing general election battle against Senator Mike Bennet. Many believe that Bennet would have lost in November to establishment GOP candidate Jane Norton. But Buck became another Tea Party underdog story, defeating Norton in the primary, not only with support from various Tea Party groups but also from a nonprofit, Americans for Job Security, which spent $2 million on ads and mailers attacking Norton.[128]

In Delaware, meanwhile, the Tea Party Express was instrumental in taking the GOP nomination away from a moderate Republican, Mike Castle. The Tea Party Express pumped in approximately $250,000 to conservative activist Christine O'Donnell's primary bid, spending it on radio and TV ads that attacked Castle's conservative credentials. The ads ran in the Philadelphia media market—where many Delaware residents work—as well as other areas of the state. Tea Party Express also garnered important endorsements of O'Donnell from conservative favorites like Sarah Palin, and the group coordinated phone banks and other volunteer activity.[129]

It worked: O'Donnell won the GOP nomination in one of the stunners of the 2010 political year. But, an unsteady candidate with extreme views, she lost handily to Democrat Chris Coons in November.

Liberal super PACs had an impact, too, on the Senate races—particularly in Washington, where liberal outside groups spent over $3 million to help Senator Patty Murray hold on to her seat. They outspent conservative groups there by about 3 to 1. Overall, though, as noted, conservative super PAC spending in 2010 generally outpaced liberal super PAC spending.[130]

In the end, the Democrats held the Senate, just barely. Currently fifty-three senators caucus with the Democrats to forty-seven for the Republicans. That would be fifty-fifty if the GOP had won the very winnable seats in Delaware, Nevada, and Colorado—all races in which independent-expenditure groups provided massive financial assistance to ideologically right-wing candidates, helping them win their party's nomination. These candidates then crashed and burned in the November general election, as many analysts (and moderate Republicans) had warned they would. Without such funding, these candidates couldn't have won their primaries.

Thus, even in its unsatisfactory (for the GOP) final result, the Senate elections of 2010 were a clear demonstration of the power of super PACs and other independent-expenditure groups.

WINNING THE HOUSE

Table 4-2 Ten Senate Races with the Most Super PAC Spending, 2010

Senate Race	Total	Liberal Groups	Conse Groups	% Liberal	% Conservative	Winner
Colorado	$9,597,547	$2,633,758	$6,963,789	27	73	Democrat
Nevada	$4,985,819	$2,003,502	$2,982,317	40	60	Democrat
Washington	$4,366,194	$3,271,818	$1,094,376	75	25	Democrat
Pennsylvania	$3,345,429	$626,392	$2,719,037	19	81	Republican
Missouri	$3,281,987	$597,968	$2,684,019	18	82	Republican
Illinois	$2,825,666	$692,128	$2,133,538	24	76	Republican
Florida	$2,730,133	$94,988	$2,635,145	3	97	Republican
Kentucky	$2,040,351	$562,611	$1,477,740	28	72	Republican
California	$1,572,560	$1,557,755	$14,805	99	1	Democrat
Alaska	$1,570,321	$0	$310,321	0	20	Republican

Lisa Murkowski won as a write-in candidate but is caucusing with Republicans.

The Democratic and Republican parties spent nearly $300 million on ads for House races in 2010—42 percent of that total financed by dollars coming from undisclosed donors.[131] Meanwhile, outside Republican groups outspent Democratic outside groups on House races, $245 million to $191 million.

American Crossroads led the way, joining in with two other pro-Republican groups— the American Action Network, the group of former senator Norm Coleman; and the Commission on Hope, Growth, and Opportunity, founded by longtime GOP campaign hand Scott Reed—to implement what it called a "House surge strategy." Down the stretch of the campaign's final three weeks, the groups spent lavishly. Crossroads laid out $10 million—on the most competitive House seats.[132]

Crossroads ran a series of ads in which it used attacks by President Obama to motivate donors. The first Crossroads ads for House races went up the week of October 11, just a little over three weeks before the election.[133] Of the twenty-seven House races on which American Crossroads and Crossroads GPS (its nonprofit arm) spent money, Republicans won fourteen.[134] In the fifteen House races that Crossroads alone invested in most heavily, its candidate prevailed in nine.

Down the stretch, American Action Network spent $19 million on twenty-two House races, winning sixteen.[135] The groups were able to target their efforts so that there was little or no overlap and money was directed for maximum utility. Thus, Republicans won thirty out of the forty-nine House races that Crossroads and AAN were involved in—a 61 percent success rate.

On the Democratic side, of course, the House results were mostly a bloodbath, but liberal independent-expenditure groups fought hard to contain the damage. America's Families First Action Fund had decent success in 2010, putting its resources into twenty-three House races and successfully influencing the outcome of seven. Three of those races were among the closest in the nation (decided by fewer than five thousand votes). Seven may not sound too good, but this was a Republican year, and Democratic losses in the House would surely have been worse without the efforts of the year's number two super PAC.[136]

Even all of the spending just documented doesn't take into account the full magnitude of independent outlays in 2010. That's because the other huge part of the puzzle is nonprofit groups—the other main beneficiaries of the *Citizens United* ruling.

●●●●●●●

NONPROFITS: SUPER PACS' DEADLY TWINS

While super PACs were the most important outgrowth of the two court decisions, they were not the only one. Readers shouldn't lose sight of the fact that the 2010 court rulings had a transformative impact on the structure and functioning of nonprofit political groups, which had existed long before these legal decisions. The rulings gave them a new lease on life: the decision in *SpeechNow.org* held that political committees making independent expenditures could accept donations unlimited in size—and that nonprofits, too, could accept unlimited contributions from corporations and unions, in addition to unlimited individual contributions.

Nonprofit political groups were now in the driver's seat: already free of FEC disclosure requirements, they now had the legal means to accept any amount of money, effectively making it open season for anyone with a political agenda to contribute to these entities. The decision also allowed the nonprofits to spend money directly on ads supporting or opposing specific candidates.

Nonprofit groups exploited their unique advantages to play a crucial role in the 2010 elections. Karl Rove and his Crossroads associates took full advantage of the opportunities that the new nonprofit landscape presented. They created a nonprofit version of American Crossroads, which they called Crossroads Grassroots Political Strategies, or GPS. Together, the two arms of American Crossroads represent a true goliath of campaign spending. As a nonprofit, Crossroads GPS is not required to disclose its donor information. American Crossroads and Crossroads GPS together have set a goal of raising $120 million for the 2012 election cycle.[137]

Overall, according to Open Secrets, all outside groups spent $293 million on the 2010 elections. About 45 percent of that total— $133 million—was spent by groups that don't have to disclose their donors.[138] In 2010, anyway, the advantage in this area was held strongly by GOP-aligned nonprofit groups. Again, this was in keeping with the fact that 2010 was a big year for Republicans, where political energies (and financial contributions) were heavily skewed toward GOP candidates and groups.

That's reflected in Table 4-3, which represents the ten Senate races in 2010 with the most nonprofit (not super PAC) spending. Conservative groups far outdid their liberal adversaries.

Table 4-3. Ten Senate Races with the Most Nonprofit Spending, 2010						
Senate Race	Total	Liberal Groups	Conservative Groups	% Liberal	% Conservative	Winner
Colorado	$8,344,151	$2,277,438	$6,052,113	27	73	Democrat
Arkansas	$7,472,940	$2,672,451	$4,800,489	36	64	Republican
Illinois	$7,116,516	$836,543	$6,279,973	12	88	Republican
Washington	$6,717,529	$1,109,760	$5,607,769	17	83	Democrat
California	$5,685,391	$212,573	$5,472,818	4	96	Democrat
Pennsylvania	$5,309,226	$1,421,100	$3,888,126	27	73	Republican
Nevada	$4,887,634	$1,023,750	$3,863,884	21	79	Democrat
Missouri	$4,791,617	$1,790,609	$3,001,008	37	63	Republican
New Hampshire	$3,993,241	$357,592	$3,635,649	9	91	Republican
Kentucky	$2,828,312	$90	$2,828,222	0	100	Republican

Given the GOP spending advantage in these races, some might point to the fact that Democrats still managed to win four out of these ten races and suggest that perhaps campaign spending isn't such a big issue after all. If Democrats could almost break even while being outspent so heavily, doesn't that suggest that other factors are at play?

Of course they are. I've never suggested that money is the *only* factor.

Further, every state and race is different—from voting demographics to quality of candidates to the condition of the local economy. Generally speaking, though, in races with relatively evenly matched candidates and an electorate about evenly split between the parties—conditions that don't pertain in every race, by any means—a big spending advantage will decide the outcome. Conversely, if your candidate is hopeless, as Sharron Angle was in Nevada, no amount of dollars is going to change the outcome.

But again, the issue isn't really about wins and losses—it's about democracy itself, about who gets to have a say in our politics, in choosing our leaders, and in having a voice in policymaking. What the super PAC universe has created is one in which the voices in this conversation are fewer and fewer, wealthier and wealthier, and holding viewpoints that are increasingly narrow and specialized to their own self-interests. It's difficult to maintain even a pretense that these independent-expenditure groups represent a public interest. They pursue private interests with private money—money that comes from a smaller and smaller core group of power players. The system is now designed to cater to their needs.

LESSONS FROM 2010

Simply put, super PACs and other independent-expenditure groups were directly responsible for the GOP's recapture of the House of Representatives. I've documented this above; it's sobering to realize how successful they were in realizing this fundamental goal, and how swamping the political system with cash delivered their desired outcome.

There is no question that super PACs have moved the Republican Party further to the right. As we've seen above, wealthy donors pumped enormous sums of cash into campaigns favoring ideologically right-wing candidates, in both House and Senate races. Their power is such, in fact, that they can shape both good outcomes and bad—as seen in those crucial three Senate races (Colorado, Nevada, and Delaware) in which right-wing candidates went down to defeats in states in which moderates likely would have won.

It also seems clear that the new super PAC landscape has emboldened unions and other traditional Democratic interest groups and strengthened their influence within the party—moving it leftward. Unions have fundraising capability that few, if any, other Democratic constituencies can match, and the new rules give them far more flexibility than they previously enjoyed. I've discussed the power of the new right-wing independent groups in influencing Republican primary battles; we should expect to see similar dynamics on the left, where unions use their clout to unseat incumbent Democrats seen as insufficiently supportive of union causes.

It's long been a truism of American politics that Senate races tend to reward more moderate candidates than do House races. Candidates can be super-conservative (or super-liberal) when they represent just a portion of a state, but it's much harder to do that when they're representing an entire state. Thus, the ideological fervor of many conservative super PACs proved potent and effective in the House races—and potent, but sometimes destructive, in the Senate races.

The Republican Party could have won the Senate in 2010 if it had won those three Senate seats—its failure to do so, however, illustrates the power of super PACs every bit as much as does its success in taking back the House.

The Republican Party has changed irrevocably since the advent of super PACs. Look at the efforts of longtime stalwart GOP senators like Orrin Hatch and Richard Lugar to fight for their political lives in the face of massive efforts by challengers funded by independent expenditures. And how have they tried to save themselves? By moving right—by attempting to convince conservative voters that they are *not* moderates. If senators of this distinction and long service need to resort to such tactics, then no Republican legislator or senator can expect to be free of such pressures.

There is no question that the 2010 elections were the dress rehearsal for what we're seeing in 2012. Liberated by the landmark court decisions, the independent-expenditure groups flooded the system with money and played an extraordinarily influential role in the races that saw a Republican recapture of the House of Representatives. No midterm election ever sees the same level of spending that presidential elections do, and so it shouldn't be surprising that political spending in 2012 has escalated far beyond the numbers in 2010. But 2010 was the most expensive midterm election in American history, with more than -á-á spent.[139]

The money war that 2010 set off hasn't stopped for a moment since. Super PAC money now dominates the presidential landscape, as Chapter 5 will detail. As this chapter was being written—in early April 2012—"403 groups organized as super PACs have reported total receipts of $153,824,830 and total independent expenditures of $84,618,524 in the 2012 cycle."[140]

Who knows what the final tally will be in terms of dollars spent? That's a matter for statisticians and others devoted to scrutinizing campaign finance. But for all other Americans, the numbers should be profoundly disturbing, because they threaten the future of our democracy. I have no hesitation in saying that in our political history, 2010 will be remembered as a watershed year. It marks the point at which the United States took a crucial step in transitioning from a citizens' democracy to a system run by and for the super-wealthy. Time will tell whether that step is irrevocable.

5

Super PACs and the 2012 GOP Primaries

"I'm against very wealthy people attempting to or influencing elections," he shrugs. "But as long as it's doable I'm going to do it. Because I know that guys like Soros have been doing it for years, if not decades. And they stay below the radar by creating a network of corporations to funnel their money. I have my own philosophy and I'm not ashamed of it. I gave the money because there is no other legal way to do it. I don't want to go through ten different corporations to hide my name. I'm proud of what I do and I'm not looking to escape recognition."

Sheldon Adelson, Forbes[141]

"He would buy an election if he could."

Newt Gingrich, on Mitt Romney[142]

On March 13, 2012, as broadcast and cable newsrooms awaited returns from the GOP primaries in Alabama and Mississippi, CNN anchor Erin Burnett flashed some astonishing figures: first, front-runner Mitt Romney's campaign had outspent, by nearly 2 to 1, the combined expenditures of the campaigns of his rivals—Rick Santorum, Newt Gingrich, and Ron Paul—on broadcast television ads (i.e., not cable) since the race had begun:

Romney	$12.4 million
Santorum	$1.5 million
Gingrich	$1.9 million
Paul	$2.9 million

But that was just the warm-up. Burnett refreshed the screen to show a more revealing graphic: total spending on broadcast TV ads by both the campaigns *and the super PACs that support them.* That measure yielded these figures:

Romney	$37.7 million
Santorum	$4.1 million
Gingrich	$7.5 million
Paul	$3.1 million

With super PAC spending included, Romney was outspending all of his rivals combined by a much better than 2-to-1 ratio.[143] That's revealing enough about the financial advantage Romney held over his GOP opponents, but the comparison also showed the outsized role super PACs played in all of the GOP campaigns (except Paul's). Super PACs are over-taking official campaigns in fundraising by a wide margin.[144] Super PAC spending was roughly two-thirds of Romney's campaign total; it was more than two-thirds of Santorum's; it was close to three-fourths of Gingrich's.

At the risk of stating the obvious here, this is a race for the American presidency we're talking about. In 2012, it is a race being paid for and controlled, overwhelmingly, by the private, unaccountable money of super PAC donors. Beyond that, the 2012 race is being controlled by one or two people who are running these super PACs and funding them.

And if there's one man who epitomizes such control, it's Sheldon Adelson—*Forbes*'s eighth wealthiest American, CEO of the Las Vegas Sands and mastermind of the Sands Macao casino in China, a venture that multiplied his wealth by a factor of 14.[145] Adelson single-handedly kept Newt Gingrich alive in the race while dividing the vote and keep-ing the race from becoming a Romney-Santorum contest much earlier. Putting it another way, a man who made much of his current fortune in Macau is now among the most important actors in American politics.

During the GOP primaries, others vied for that role: investment manager Foster Friess, for example, who donated approximately $1 mil-lion to the Red White and Blue Fund, the super PAC supporting Rick Santorum. Friess, a passionate advocate of conservative Christian causes, played a crucial role in keeping Santorum alive in the race. The former Pennsylvania senator's campaign had languished throughout 2011, but with the support of Friess, he was able to build momentum and become the final obstacle for Romney on his way to the Republican nomination.

Super PACs have taken over American politics. They not only far outspend the official campaigns on political advertising; they dominate the political process and decision making. Candidates' campaigns increasingly defer to super PACs; in Romney's case, for example, the campaign pulled back and spent its ample (but finite) advertising dollars in locations where it would be most effective—leaving the Romney-supporting super PAC, Restore Our Future, to flood other outlets with advertising dollars.

For those who feared the impact super PACs would have on American politics in the wake of the *Citizens United* ruling, the 2012 GOP presidential race provides all the evidence needed. In a topsy-turvy primary, in which no candidate could sustain his momentum, there was one reliable constant: super PAC money would write the storyline.

Eventually, an overwhelming edge in super PAC dollars would propel Mitt Romney to the GOP nomination. Romney's crucial victories in Michigan, Ohio, and Illinois were directly and inexorably linked to super PAC advertising—*overwhelmingly negative advertising*. According to the *Washington Post*, Romney's Restore Our Future PAC devoted an astounding *92 percent of its ad spending—$24.5 million—to negative ads*.[146] (Rick Santorum's Red White Blue Fund was no slouch at 84 percent, but the funding discrepancy here is pivotal—RWBF laid out just $3 million, total, on such ads. It's pretty difficult to compete with someone who is out-attacking you at an 8-to-1 financial spending clip.) Restore Our Future accounted for 83 percent of all negative spending in the GOP primaries.[147]

Negative ads are not only damaging for the tone they send—they're also often deceptive or dishonest. Restore Our Future led the pack in this respect, too. According to an Annenberg Public Policy Center study, $23.3 million of the $41.1 million spent from the time of the Iowa caucuses to the end of the Wisconsin primary went toward deceptive attacks—and Restore Our Future accounted for nearly all of that sum.[148]

A candidate as flawed as Romney, with so much demonstrated difficulty in rallying the Republican base, would never have survived without super PACs.

●●●●●●●

IOWA CAUCUSES

Iowa immediately made clear how dominant super PACs would be. Super PAC spending, especially on negative ads, shaped and reshaped the race, and total political expenditures set a new state record of $12 million—an estimated two-thirds of it from super PACs. "It's hard to figure out who is doing the attacking and to what end, and they're double-barreling the attacks on two or more candidates," said journalist David Yepsen, who covered nine Iowa caucuses for the *Des Moines Register*. "I've never seen that before. We've never had this volume [of negative ads] or this much complexity."[149]

"He would buy an election if he could," Newt Gingrich said of his rival Mitt Romney before the Iowa caucuses,[150] and for many, Gingrich's warning came true. In Iowa, where Gingrich once held a double-digit lead, he was beaten by Santorum and Romney—mostly due to the impact of a blizzard of negative ads paid for by Restore Our Future, the Romney-supporting super PAC whose largest contributor so far is John Paulson, "a New York hedge fund billionaire who became famous for enriching himself by betting on the collapse of the housing industry," according to Politico.com.[151] If it weren't for the deep-pocketed negative-ad push, Gingrich likely would have held on and won the caucus.

During the month of December, for instance, 45 percent of the political ads aired in Iowa were anti-Gingrich ads, mainly put out by super PACs supporting Romney and Rick Perry. Only about 6 percent of the ads were pro-Gingrich. Media analysts estimated that viewers in Iowa's largest media markets, Cedar Rapids–Waterloo and Des Moines, saw anti-Gingrich ads between sixty and eighty times per week.

Restore Our Future began spending aggressively on December 8, with a $782,052.49 anti-Gingrich media buy. Four days later, ROF spent another $114,134 on an anti-Gingrich media buy. On December 16, it spent $1 million on another anti-Gingrich media buy. ROF's last Iowa expenditure came on December 27, a $997,485.32 media buy opposing Perry and Gingrich, but mainly focused on Gingrich.

One of ROF's more effective anti-Gingrich ads in Iowa suggested that President Obama would be happy to run in November against the former House Speaker, who had "more baggage than the airlines." The ad effectively played on concerns about Gingrich's electability, and it went on to attack him for consulting for Freddie Mac, teaming up with Nancy Pelosi on several issues, and using taxpayer dollars to help fund abortions and a UN program that supported China's one-child policy. Another ad attacked both Perry and Gingrich for supporting "amnesty" for illegal immigrants and concluded by reminding viewers of Gingrich's ethics violations as Speaker of the House.

How effective were these ads? Gingrich reached a polling high in Iowa of 31 percent on December 11, when he led the race, according to the website Real Clear Politics (RCP), which maintains a running average of the presidential candidates' polling; by January 1, he had crashed to 13.8 percent. That's about where he ended up. Gingrich got just 13 percent of the vote on January 3, finishing in fourth place, 8 points behind third-place finisher Ron Paul. It's true that the month of December also saw a mainstream media onslaught against Gingrich, with reporters dredging up his checkered political history, and even explicit rejections of his candidacy by establishment conservative organs like *National Review*. But Iowa is a very independent-minded place, and candidates have won there before despite similar media barrages. Without the super PAC assault, Gingrich would have won Iowa—with who knows what impact on the GOP race.

Rick Santorum, who narrowly won Iowa, was unscathed by the negative super PAC spending because little was spent directly opposing him in the closing days of the race. He'd come from far back in the field and hadn't been the focus of any candidate's opposition spending. Santorum did, however, benefit from positive spending by the Red White and Blue Fund, the super PAC that supported him. Between December 14 and December 29, RWBF spent roughly $580,000 on pro-Santorum ads in Iowa. Did it make a difference? Consider: on December 14, the RCP average had Santorum at 5.8 percent; the highest he'd gotten at that point, before his spending surge, was 8 percent in a Public Policy Polling (PPP) survey conducted between December 11 and December 13.[152] By December 29, after two weeks of super PAC ad buys, Santorum had bumped up to 16.3 percent, and he ended up winning the caucus with 24.6 percent of the vote, thirty-four votes ahead of Mitt Romney.

After Iowa, the first primary of the season took place in New

Hampshire, a state most had already conceded to Romney. Unlike other states discussed here, New Hampshire saw comparatively little participation from outside funding groups. Romney won overwhelmingly with 39 percent of the vote, far ahead of the second-place finisher, Ron Paul, who took 22 percent.

SOUTH CAROLINA

Just as super PACs helped destroy Gingrich in Iowa, they revived him in South Carolina, where super PACs outspent the candidates' campaigns by 2-to-1.[153] Pro-Gingrich spending in South Carolina by Winning Our Future, which was almost exclusively anti-Romney, began on January 1 with an ad buy worth over $1.6 million. These ads mainly focused on attacking Romney but also supported Gingrich.

On January 7 came the biggest news of the campaign: that Sheldon Adelson had made a $5 million donation to Winning Our Future. That set the super PAC on a spending spree that ended on January 18 with over $200,000 of radio and television ads. To get a sense of how vital Adelson's intervention was, a CNN–*Time* poll for January 4–5 had Gingrich at 18 percent and Romney at 37 percent in South Carolina. A little over two weeks later, in the last poll taken before the primary, by PPP, Gingrich had reached 37 percent support while Romney had plunged to 28 percent—a truly astonishing turnaround in such a short time. Gingrich would go on to win South Carolina by an even wider margin, taking 40.4 percent of the vote compared to just 27.9 percent of the vote for Romney.

Winning Our Future helped make it happen not only with radio and TV ads but also by paying for the production of an anti-Romney documentary, *King of Bain*, a twenty-eight-minute attack on Mitt Romney's career at Bain Capital, which alleged that Romney was more responsible for killing jobs than creating them. The online film, aside from not being terribly accurate—the *Washington Post* gave it its lowest ranking, a full four Pinocchios[154]—was also widely criticized by the conservative punditry as an attack against free-market capitalism. Others noted that it essentially gave President Obama a playbook to use in ads against Romney, which eventually happened.[155] Perhaps most important of all, the film represented the kind of standard that super PAC advertising has increasingly shown—one that places little value on factual rigor. As Steve Coll wrote in *The New Yorker*:

> *It is not journalism, but it is not the worst piece of demagoguery that we are likely to endure before November, either, about Romney or Obama. Like most political speech and argument in the super PAC era, "King of Bain" is a narrative of noise and emotional manipulation, intercut with jagged shards of truth.*[156]

But truth in the super PAC universe is distinctly secondary to victory, and Gingrich's resounding South Carolina win reshuffled the GOP race. Counted out twice already—in summer 2011, when he fired most of his campaign team, and then after his Iowa fade—Gingrich, with Adelson's generous support, had once again clawed his way back into the race. And now Romney faced the pressure of the primary in Florida, a major electoral prize in November and a state he couldn't afford to lose.

FLORIDA

In Florida, Romney and Restore Our Future took no chances. Determined to ensure that he not be knocked off stride with a damaging loss, the candidate and the super PAC poured resources into the Sunshine State. Restore Our Future would pump $15.3 million into ads designed to take down Gingrich in Florida. That sum alone surpassed the amount ($11 million) that John McCain spent on ads for the *entire 2008 primary race.*[157] And it dwarfed the paltry $3 million Gingrich was able to muster in the state. Romney's 5-to-1 spending advantage, meanwhile, was devoted almost entirely to negative ads directed at Gingrich.

An astounding 96 percent of all Florida ads were negative, and 68 percent of those were specifically targeted against Gingrich. Although Restore Our Future began spending in Florida early with a $287,250 media buy on December 16, it only began spending in earnest on January 11, when it spent over $1.7 million on another media buy (directed against Gingrich). The ads were both ubiquitous and aggressive.

One ad, which also aired in South Carolina, lambasted Gingrich for his attacks on Romney, and cited conservative organizations' criticisms of Gingrich's attacks as "foolish," "out of bounds," and "disgusting." It repeated the "airline baggage" line from Iowa, and again hit Gingrich for his ethics violations, his work for Freddie Mac, and his cooperation with Nancy Pelosi on the bill supporting the one-child policy. Don't be fooled by Gingrich's "desperate attacks," the ad warns viewers. Another ad argued that Gingrich was unelectable, an issue known to have significance among Romney-leaning voters. Even when the ads seemed a bit petty—especially the one contrasting Gingrich's mention of Ronald Reagan over fifty times in the debates with Reagan's lone mention of Gingrich, in passing, in his presidential diaries—their consistent negative assault on the former Speaker's record and character did lasting damage.

To understand how much damage, one has only to consult the polling. According to the Real Clear Politics average, Gingrich started out the new year ahead of Romney in Florida by a wide margin—38.3 percent to 26.3 percent. By the end of January, after the bulk of super PAC spending, Romney was leading Gingrich, 41.8 percent to 28.8 percent. On January 31, Romney won Florida by 14.5 points, taking 46.4 percent of the vote to Gingrich's 31.9 percent. For the time being, he was back on top, reclaiming his front-runner's mantle.

The big question coming out of Florida, at least in terms of super PACs, was: where was Adelson's money? If Adelson was willing to pump $5 million at one swoop into Gingrich's campaign, why wasn't he willing to spend more in Florida—especially given the success Gingrich had had in South Carolina and the enormous spending Romney was doing? Some Gingrich insiders say that money *was* pumped in, while others suggest that Gingrich himself was conflicted over how negative to be in his Florida advertising—having won in South Carolina, he felt the need to be more "presidential." Others say that there was internal division in the campaign over what kinds of ads to run, and where.

Whatever the real story, the results are clear: by neglecting to spend money on the kind of all-out TV blitz that he'd purchased in South Carolina, Adelson cost Gingrich his last chance to knock out Romney and become the GOP nominee. By their presence and their absence, super PAC dollars determined the Florida winner.

It wasn't clear right away, but the Florida results also signaled the next shift in the race. Gingrich from here on would be a bit player—though an important one—and Rick Santorum would eventually rise to the fore as the latest, and the last, anti-Romney candidate. This became clear on February 7, when Santorum swept to caucus victories in Minnesota and Colorado and a nonbinding primary win in Missouri. By mid- and late February, Santorum was surging in polls ahead of two crucial primaries on February 28: Michigan and Arizona.

In total, super PACs spent $5.8 million in Michigan and Arizona. The vast majority of this, 85 percent, was spent in Michigan. Romney's Restore Our Future was the only super PAC to invest seriously in Arizona, spending $660,000. By comparison, Gingrich's Winning Our Future spent just $230,000, to no discernible effect; in fact, Gingrich ended up performing more poorly than expected. Yet this seemingly minor investment by ROF—trifling compared with what was spent in other states—had a dramatic effect on the outcome in Arizona. Again, the story is told in the polling.

On February 20, eight days before the primary, Romney's support in the polls had dropped from a high of 44.5 percent to 37.5 percent, while Santorum had come from 13.5 percent to second place at 32 percent, according to the RCP average. The Santorum surge was picking up momentum. On February 21, Restore Our Future spent $334,849.68 on a media buy, saturating the airwaves with anti-Santorum ads in the coming days. By election night, Santorum's Arizona momentum had been stopped in its tracks, and RCP projected Romney winning in a rout, 42.8 percent to 27.3 percent. He did better than that, winning the state by 20 points, 47 percent to Santorum's 27 percent.

It's likely that other super PACs—like Santorum's Red White and Blue Fund—didn't invest in Arizona because the state, in violation of RNC rules, was making its primary a winner-take-all instead of proportional contest, meaning that they'd have nothing to show for their investment unless they won outright. Still, before Restore Our Future's cash injection intervened, Santorum was closing fast on Romney.

Michigan was much more competitive. At first, it looked like a comfortable win for Romney in his native state. Rasmussen polling showed Romney up by 15 points in Michigan on February 1, but that was before Santorum's caucus sweep. By February 12, a PPP poll showed the former Pennsylvania senator leading by 15 points. On February 15, Santorum had, in two days, jumped from 14 percent support in Michigan to 37.8 percent, while Romney had dropped from 33 percent to 29 percent, the first time he had fallen below 30 percent. Santorum's caucus victories were encouraging, but a victory in a populous battleground state like Michigan would give him a legitimate claim as a viable nominee.

Until February 19, polls showed Santorum in the lead in Michigan by margins ranging from 3 to 10 points. However, after February 19, Romney began to rise in the polls, coming out on top in eight of the last twelve polls to be released before the election. Let's follow the money: on February 14, Restore Our Future spent $869,799.32 in media buys and began hammering Santorum with negative ads, apparently blunting his momentum over just five days. Then, on February 21, ROF spent nearly $1 million on Internet advertising and a media buy attacking Santorum.[158] The next day, ROF spent over $500,000 on another anti-Santorum media buy. Over the last two weeks of the Michigan race, 100 percent of Restore Our Future's spending went toward anti-Santorum ads.[159]

"More than twenty years in Washington has changed Rick Santorum's values," intoned one pro-Romney ad, using as evidence his vote to give violent felons the right to cast ballots, his vote to raise the U.S. debt limit five times, and his stated pride in the billions in earmarks he had brought home to Pennsylvania. Another ad that aired in Michigan—and Arizona and Ohio—used a similar line of attack, concluding with a memorable description of Santorum: "Big spender. Washington insider." Santorum countered with an effective ad that attacked Romney for his millions in negative ads. Here's how one prominent spot was described:

"Mitt Romney's negative attack machine is back, on full throttle. This time, Romney's firing his mud at Rick Santorum," says the voice-over. Those lines play over a scene of an actor who looks like Romney wielding a mud-slinging gun and hunting cardboard cutouts of Santorum in a warehouse. The voice goes on: "Romney and his super PAC have spent a staggering twenty million attacking fellow Republicans. Why? Because Romney's trying to hide from his big-government Romneycare, and his support for job-killing cap-and-trade. And in the end, Mitt Romney's ugly attacks are going to backfire."[160]

But however effective his ads were, Santorum was simply outgunned in Michigan. In total, Restore Our Future invested $2.9 million in Michigan, while Santorum's Red White and Blue Fund put in $1.7 million. All told, Romney's campaign spending plus ROF spending totaled $4.2 million in Michigan, nearly twice that of the Santorum campaign and super PAC.[161] Showing serious momentum and presenting a genuine threat to Romney's candidacy, Santorum ran into a buzz saw of super PAC money. When the chips were down in Michigan, Romney's super PAC made the difference, pounding the Santorum campaign into submission.

On February 28, Romney won Michigan by 3.2 points, 41.1 percent to 37.9 percent.

●●●●●●●

SUPER TUESDAY: MARCH 6, 2012

Romney's narrow escape in Michigan made the Super Tuesday races all the more vital. Primaries or caucuses would be held in Alaska, Georgia, Idaho, Massachusetts, North Dakota, Oklahoma, Tennessee, Vermont, Virginia, and Wyoming—but most of the attention centered on Ohio, the battleground state of all battleground states, the elector of presidents. As with previous milestone states like Florida and Michigan, super PACs would crucially shape the storyline, and the result, in Ohio.

Before discussing the Ohio race, it's important to note a broader trend exemplified by the Super Tuesday races: the growing ability of super PACs to outspend the campaigns themselves. In the two weeks leading up to the March 6 Super Tuesday elections, super PACs outspent campaigns by a margin of more than 3 to 1—$7.85 million to $2.4 million. For the leading candidate, the disparity was even more pronounced: in the last week leading up to Super Tuesday, Romney's campaign was outspent more than 6 to 1 by his super PAC, Restore Our Future. In the final two weeks in Ohio, the Romney campaign spent $1.5 million to Restore Our Future's $1.7 million. With Santorum, the disparity was less extreme but still impressive: his Red White and Blue Fund outspent his campaign in Ohio by nearly 3 to 1 in Ohio in the final two weeks.162

Gingrich relied almost exclusively on his Winning Our Future PAC, which spent $770,000 on his behalf in Ohio. Winning Our Future also spent a combined $3.1 million in Ohio, Tennessee, Oklahoma, and Georgia; his campaign spent just $45,000 on TV ads in those four states combined.163 And while Romney's campaign did not air one ad outside of Ohio, Restore Our Future spent $900,000 in Georgia, $750,000 in Tennessee, and $400,000 in Oklahoma—a combined $2.05 million.

OHIO

As the campaigning in Ohio kicked off in earnest, Santorum retained significant momentum. His loss in Michigan had been so narrow, in a state where Romney had grown up and which his father had served as governor, and he had been so massively outspent there, that he could still credibly claim a serious shot at the nomination. Santorum's social conservatism would have broad appeal in Ohio, especially outside of its main urban areas like Cleveland and Cincinnati. Many saw Romney's shaky hold on the nomination facing its most serious test in Ohio, and all of the early polls indicated that this was the case.

For example, a Rasmussen poll, conducted on February 15, had Santorum trouncing Romney, 42 percent to 24 percent. That poll might have skewed Santorum's way to some degree, but other polls bore out his lead: the RCP average had him surging between February 12 and February 16, when his support in Ohio jumped from 20 percent to 33 percent. Two polls, one conducted by the University of Cincinnati between February 16 and February 22, and another by Quinnipiac, conducted between February 23 and February 26, had Santorum leading by 11 and 7 points, respectively. As late as February 27, the RCP average in Ohio had Santorum solidly ahead, 33.3 percent to Romney's 26 percent.

That's when Restore Our Future got busy. The super PAC spent over $5.2 million that week, 81 percent of which was directed against Santorum. One week later, the RCP average had Romney just nosing out Santorum in a statistical dead heat, 33.5 percent to 33.3 percent. By March 5, the day before Super Tuesday, polls released by Quinnipiac and PPP showed Romney leading by 3 percent and 1 percent, respectively; a previous Quinnipiac poll taken four days earlier showed Santorum up by 4 percent. A Rasmussen poll still showed Santorum up by 1 percent. Clearly, the vote would be razor-close; just as clearly, the Romney campaign—and especially Restore Our Future—had turned the Ohio race around in just a week.

Restore Our Future would outspend Santorum's Red White and Blue fund in Ohio by 3 to 1. The ROF push was heavily loaded toward the campaign's last two weeks. On February 22, it spent $760,735.19 on a media buy opposing Santorum, and $176,084 on Internet advertising attacking both Gingrich and Santorum, but mainly Santorum. On February 28, it spent another $277,629 on an anti-Santorum media buy. On February 29, Restore Our Future spent over $1 million on a media buy focused on attacking Santorum.

In an ad appearing in Ohio, Oklahoma, and Tennessee, Restore Our Future blasted Santorum for voting for a bill that included funding for Planned Parenthood even after he said it violated his personal moral convictions. The Restore Our Future ads followed a pattern: they revisited various positions taken by Romney's opponents—either in the form of votes, bill sponsorships, or television quotes—and used them to criticize the candidate's character. For example, an ad that ran in Michigan criticizing Santorum for wasteful spending and earmarks ended by saying: "More than twenty years in Washington has changed Rick Santorum's values." Another pointed out how Santorum had voted to increase his salary in Congress.

The ROF ads were almost uniformly negative, for which Romney was often criticized. But they usually worked. Out of the over $31 million spent by ROF, 97 percent of those dollars went toward attack ads. In fact, ROF has spent barely $1 million to date on positive ads. By contrast, Winning Our Future spent just a quarter of its $16 million in expenditures on attack ads. Still, ROF's tendency is more typical of super PACs as a whole: super PACs have sponsored more negative than positive ads in every state except for New Hampshire (30 percent on negative ads), Idaho (42 percent), and Minnesota (50 percent).

Faced with the ROF onslaught, the Red White and Blue Fund tried to fight back. From February 21 through February 24, the super PAC spent nearly half a million dollars on voter-contact mail supporting Santorum and attacking Romney. On February 24, it purchased $257,061 of television ads supporting Santorum and attacking Romney and Gingrich. Red White and Blue's last spending push was an identical TV buy on March 1.

At the same time, Gingrich's Winning Our Future PAC made its presence felt—reflecting a shift in strategy by Adelson. While recognizing that Gingrich was no longer a serious threat to win the nomination, the billionaire refused to take his stake out of the race. Perhaps more than wanting Gingrich to win, he now feared a Santorum candidacy. Adelman loathed the former Pennsylvania senator's positions on social issues, and so he kept Gingrich bankrolled, assuring that the anti-Romney vote would be split and preventing a one-on-one, Romney versus Santorum showdown.

One Winning Our Future ad showed clips of interviews with everyday people who call Romney "un-relatable" and asking whether or not he is "strong enough to beat Obama." Another woman says that Romney is "unreliable," that she "cannot understand what he stands for," and that "we're looking at $5, $6 gas, and Romney's not the type to pump his own gas." (She says this as a picture of Romney entering a private jet flashes on the screen.) The ad also serves as a positive Gingrich ad, not just an attack ad.

But neither Red White and Blue nor Winning Our Future had the resources to derail the express train of money that Restore Our Future brought into Ohio. By primary day, the RCP average projected Romney winning Ohio by 1.2 points. It would be even closer than that, with Romney winning 37.9 to Santorum's 37.1. "We didn't win by a lot, but we won by enough, and that's what counts," Romney told his supporters that evening. He was right; the Ohio win was the most important of the primary season.

Without super PACs, Romney never could have done it.

ALABAMA AND MISSISSIPPI

Super Tuesday was a good night for Romney. A loss in Ohio would have upended the race, but Santorum remained a serious threat. And with two deeply conservative states, Alabama and Mississippi, next on the primary calendar, Santorum stood a good chance to score some victories. Polls showed a close race between the three main candidates in both states. Gingrich, being the only Southerner, was thought to have a better chance than in some recent states.

The now-familiar pattern of super PAC funding dominance continued in both Deep South states, where the various super PACs paid for almost all television advertising: 91 percent of the 5,592 campaign ads that aired in the month before the voting began. The numbers once again tell the story, and Romney's Restore Our Future by far outpaced its competitors. The super PAC aired 65 percent of *all* ads in the two states, according to advertising-tracking firm CMAG. Restore Our Future paid for 1,548 ads in Mississippi, compared with 454 for Winning Our Future and 300 for Red White and Blue, according to CMAG.

ROF's efforts far outpaced those of the Romney campaign: the super PAC aired ads 2,098 times in Alabama before the final two days of the campaign—compared with just 279 spots paid for by his campaign. Gingrich's Winning Our Future ran 411 ad spots in Alabama; his official campaign put up only 131. Santorum's campaign aired no broadcast ads at all in Alabama—but the Red White and Blue Fund ran 282 spots on his behalf.[164]

On March 13, Santorum took both states. He won Alabama with 34.5 percent of the vote to Gingrich's 29.3 and Romney's 29 percent, and he prevailed in Mississippi with 32.8 to Gingrich's 31.2 and Romney's 30.6. These losses represent almost the only time that a Romney effort went down to defeat when his super PAC was so far outspending its competitors—but it should be put in context. Santorum's wins here didn't constitute what pundits call a "game changer." The candidate was a natural for these two deeply southern states, where the kind of social conservatism dreaded by Sheldon Adelson exerts something like a gravitational pull. Super PACs may not—yet—be able to alter gravity, but in the GOP race, they shaped pretty much everything else, much to the relief of Mitt Romney.

· · ● ● ● ● ● ● · ·

ILLINOIS AND THE END GAME

The GOP primary battle was finally joined in Illinois. Observers saw a good chance for Santorum here, especially given the state's southern and western portions, which are much more socially conservative than Chicago and its affluent suburbs, which were expected to go for Romney. Santorum had fallen short in Ohio and Michigan; like those states, Illinois was a state that could confer full-scale legitimacy on Santorum if he could win it. Likewise, for Romney, a loss here would weaken further his claim to being the inevitable GOP nominee.

What seemed like a stage for a serious battle, however, soon grew out of reach for Santorum, and for one undeniable reason: Romney's campaign and super PAC outspent Santorum's campaign and his super PAC, combined, by 7 to 1: $3.5 million for Romney versus a little over $500,000 for Santorum. In the media-saturated Chicago market, meanwhile, that edge exponentially rose to *21 to 1*: $2 million for Romney versus just $97,119 for Santorum.[165] Increasingly priced out of such expensive ad markets, the Red White and Blue Fund avoided ad buys in Chicago and instead spent its funds in smaller, cheaper markets, like Champaign-

Urbana, Peoria, and Rockford.[166] The problem with that strategy was twofold: first, Santorum desperately needed to counter Romney's spending in Chicago; second, his penny-pinching in that market didn't bode well for his ability to spend in California and New York, where ads were even pricier.

In fact, Romney's super PAC spending so dwarfed his opponents' in Illinois—Gingrich spent just $17,000 there—that, as Paul Blumenthal wrote in the *Huffington Post*, Restore Our Future has come to be known as the Death Star.[167]

You don't need to be a political scientist to understand the significance of those spending disparities. And sure enough, on election night, they yielded a predictable result: Romney carried the state decisively, 47 percent to 35 percent. It was his most clear-cut victory in an important state during the primary season, and for many in the GOP establishment, it sparked a chorus of unity and another attempt at rallying the party to a Romney candidacy. This time, it worked: the party began falling in behind Romney, and the rest of the primary campaign became smooth sailing for the now presumptive GOP nominee.

Romney would go on to win primary contests in Maryland, Wisconsin, and the District of Columbia. Santorum, seeing the writing on the wall, low on cash, and facing a difficult family situation with his ailing young daughter, dropped out on April 10. Romney then went on to sweep the April 24 primaries in Connecticut, Delaware, New York, Pennsylvania, and Rhode Island. Romney clinched the nomination on May 29, when he won the Texas primary and reached the required 1,144 delegates. It hasn't been easy, but Romney has gotten what he sought: the GOP nomination and a fall showdown with President Obama.

WHAT TO EXPECT IN THE GENERAL ELECTION

The way that super PAC spending has come to dwarf official campaign spending in many states indicates not just their obvious political and financial clout but also the campaigns' own understanding of the new dynamics of election financing. Romney's campaign, especially, showed a keen awareness of how to leverage Restore Our Future across many states while conserving its own limited resources. The Romney campaign spent money only where it was most effective, leaving it to Restore Our Future to spend the largest share of advertising dollars. This approach offered many advantages: first, conserving its own money; second, giving itself a shot everywhere, through the super PAC dollars; and third, having easy "deniability" in states where it didn't fare well, by pointing to its own limited expenditures and claiming that it never thought it could win there anyway (even as the "independent" super PAC flooded money in).

But for an onslaught of negative ads in each state, overwhelming Santorum's expenditures by better than 2 to 1 or 3 to 1 at the lowest end—and much more than that in states like Illinois—Mitt Romney might well have lost at least two or three crucial states, potentially fundamentally altering the outcome of the 2012 Republican primary nominating contest. Such enormous bankrolling—by unaccountable sources—of almost solely negative advertising is simply unprecedented in our campaigns. And apparently, given how tenacious the contest has been, Romney needed every penny. He has the Supreme Court and *Citizens United* to thank for the GOP nomination.

Think about it this way: in a race for one of the two major party's presidential nomination, events and outcomes were shaped by a casino magnate (Adelson), a social-issues zealot (Friess), and about thirty hedge-fund managers. Has our democracy become an oligarchy? Considering that somewhere between thirty and fifty men are now controlling our political process, the answer to that question is not a happy one. At best, we've become a frighteningly unrepresentative democracy, our politics corrupted and shadowy, perhaps beyond repair.

6

●●●●●●●

Why 2012 Will Be the Nastiest, Costliest Race in History

We're also going to be prepared, and I want to be clear, to respond to the attacks that we expect to continue from—not just from the Romney campaign but from the Karl [Rove] and Koch brothers, contract killers over there in super PAC land, who are going to continue to pound away on behalf of Governor Romney. We will respond vigorously.

David Axelrod, May 7, 2012[168]

Voices not belonging to the candidates are now the primary voices driving the dialogue in political campaigns.

Steve Schmidt, GOP strategist, May 17, 2012[169]

As this book was being finalized, the 2012 general election was just beginning to gear up. Technically, the Republican primary process remains ongoing, with state primaries on the calendar until June. But barring some unforeseen event of unimaginable magnitude, Mitt Romney will be the GOP nominee and face off against President Obama in the fall. It is impossible to predict, of course, what will transpire between now and then, and what unexpected developments will shape the campaign—to say nothing of predicting a winner.

I did not write this book to make predictions, however, but rather to make an argument about the role of money in politics, particularly in the wake of recent court decisions and the evolution of super PACs. With that in mind, and after observing what super PACs and other outside groups have already done this year, I think there are a number of observations to make about the 2012 campaign that will remain valid no matter what the eventual outcome in November.

With a high degree of certainty, I believe we can expect to see three things this election cycle: increasingly negative and expensive campaigns; Republicans relying on super PACs and megadonors and Democrats relying on unions; and an even more limited and beclouded disclosure process for donations.

No one questions that the 2012 election will be the most expensive in American history. The Obama campaign alone is expected to raise around $1 billion;170 and the Romney campaign has a target of $800 million.[171] These are just the *official* campaigns. Karl Rove's network of organizations, all under the Crossroads banner, are expected to spend up to $300 million to help elect Republicans across the country,[172] while unions are expected to spend $400 million or more to help Democrats.[173] The

Rove-led American Crossroads, along with other conservative groups, are determined to recapture the Senate in 2012—just as they recaptured the House in 2010.

By mid-May, with the in-earnest campaign still in its infancy, we got a powerful indication of the impact super PACs will have in the campaign.

The Obama campaign announced a $25 million ad campaign touting the president's record; almost immediately, Crossroads GPS announced an equivalent $25 million expenditure on television ads attacking the president.[174] Steve Schmidt, chief strategist to McCain's 2008 campaign whom I quote at the outset of this chapter, noted that as a Republican partisan, he was happy with the way events were unfolding. As an American, however, he was troubled, and his concern bears repeating: "Voices not belonging to the candidates are now the primary voices driving the dialogue in political campaigns," he said.[175]

These outside voices can take the dialogue just about anywhere—and as another mid-May episode showed, that includes racially negative advertisements.

As the *New York Times* reported, Joe Ricketts, patriarch of the Chicago Cubs–owning Ricketts family, is the main financer behind Ending Spending Action Fund, a super PAC. He was said to be considering a plan, presented to him by his group, that proposed to attack President Obama on his ties to the Reverend Jeremiah Wright. Furthermore, the ads' narrator would call the president a "metrosexual, black Abe Lincoln." Thankfully, once the story broke, the plan was rejected.[176]

Speaking frankly, racially divisive negative advertisements of this sort do not belong in a presidential election. Whether one supports the president or not, he should be judged on his record—on which there is plenty to argue about, pro and con. Ad hominem attacks of any sort should have no home in the public arena. It is more than just disquieting that $10 million was almost allocated to fund ads that threatened to kindle racial tensions and call the president a "metrosexual";[177] it is also shameful and embarrassing.

The Ricketts episode (and I doubt we've heard the last of him or his group, by the way) illustrates one of the core dangers of super PACs: how readily they make possible these kinds of attacks by giving the extremely wealthy, and sometimes unhinged, the ability to steer the narrative of an election—independently of larger party frameworks or any oversight at all. Putting it another way, super PACs allow anyone rich enough to unilaterally drag the entire election into the mire, creating scenarios that are more than just offensive or strange, but truly absurd.

Rahm Emmanuel, former White House chief of staff and now mayor of Chicago, best expressed my sentiments. Of the attacks, he said: "I don't think that's fitting in a campaign of any nature. . . . America is too great a country with too great a future." He's right: America *is* too great a country, with too noble a democratic history, to let our most important election fall into such a divisive spiral. Allowing super PACs so much control over our elections, as Emmanuel says, is "insulting to the country."[178]

Perhaps this makes me a bit of an anachronism, but I still firmly believe that a presidential campaign is supposed to be a dialogue—or a spirited battle—between the two campaigns and parties. Super PACs change the equation so that elections are more about candidates and their henchmen *responding* to moves made by outside groups. This is really a paradigmatic shift in the American political landscape, and from the perspective of someone who has inhabited that terrain for the better part of his life, it's a bizarre and frightening one.

Consider how David Axelrod took time in a conference call to call Karl Rove (behind the Crossroads franchise) and the Koch brothers (financers of Americans for Prosperity) super PAC "contract killers." It is one thing that a former senior advisor to the president and top aide to his campaign devotes time to attacking two outside groups. Talk is cheap. It is something entirely different that he announces the campaign will spend $25 million in the month of May—an early, relatively quiet month in presidential campaigns—to respond to those super PACs.[179] The Obama campaign's $25 million, what some have called a "nuclear bomb," is being spent to push back against the anti-Obama narrative with which conservative super PACS have been trying to frame the election. The campaign's investment clearly illustrates how fundamentally campaign dynamics have changed and how effective super PACs have become in shaping and driving strategy.

So super PACs have forced the hand of the best-organized, most well-funded campaign in American history. Would the Obama campaign find it necessary to spend $25 million in one month—six months before voters go to the polls—if super PACs weren't having the impact they're having? The magnitude of the response indicates that the president and his campaign are worried.

And they have good cause to be: while the official Obama campaign will probably outraise Romney, the GOP holds a significant edge in super PAC fundraising. This is the challenge that the Obama reelection team now faces.

What makes this situation unique and even more dangerous is that there is no Democratic super PAC able to challenge Crossroads. This in effect forces the Obama campaign to deal directly with super PACs and not subcontract that task to its own outside groups. For the first time ever, a completely independent, unaccountable outside group, partially funded by undisclosed donors, is the main engine of debate.

●●●●●●●●●

THE GOP'S SUPER PAC ADVANTAGE

Already, groups like Crossroads, the Chamber of Commerce, and Americans for Prosperity are pumping money into negative ads in states with key Senate races—like Missouri, where incumbent Democrat Claire McCaskill has been attacked with over $2 million in negative ads. The Chamber of Commerce expects to exceed its $30 million investment in 2010; it will be, according to officials, "the most significant political effort" in the organization's history. Crossroads estimates that it will spend $60 million on Senate races and $30 million on House races.[180]

The effect of introducing unlimited sources of funding to an already well-funded, hypercompetitive, hyperpartisan, high-stakes system exacerbates all the system's worst tendencies. Super PACs not only compete with one another—increasingly focusing their attention on small cohorts of the extremely rich; they also spark greater spending from the official campaigns. The result will be elections and candidates increasingly influenced by megadonors, and less by average Americans.

As elections become more expensive, the ability to secure hundreds of millions of dollars will become a prerequisite for running for president; super donors will effectively control elections.

Who are these affluent folks able to make six- and seven-figure donations? We may never know fully. A number of large donors have shielded their identity by forming shell corporations and through them donating to super PACs. Furthermore, the groups themselves are able to manipulate the rules to avoid disclosure. In 2006, groups that didn't disclose their donors accounted for just 1 percent of outside spending. By May 2011, that number was at 47 percent, and I predict that by the end of this election, it will be even higher.[181]

The pro-Romney super PAC, Restore Our Future, although being primarily funded by a small cabal of wealthy donors—Wall Street types and executives—was the most "democratic" of all the GOP super PACs. Winning Our Future, the Gingrich super PAC, was almost entirely funded by the fervently pro-Israel casino mogul Sheldon Adelson, while Rick Santorum's Red White and Blue Fund survived due to the largesse of investor and social-issues zealot Foster Friess. The GOP primary has proven that one super-rich donor can highjack an election and make a candidate beholden to him.

The GOP primaries have also made clear that, at least on the presidential level, the Republicans figure to hold a strong super PAC advantage this year. Obama faces a huge and potentially fatal disadvantage: his campaign has had trouble raising super PAC money and is certainly not doing so at anywhere near the rate the Republicans are.182 Mega-rich liberal individuals are, at least so far, hesitant to give to super PACs. Although the Obama campaign initially had a 10-to-1 financial advantage over the Romney campaign, Romney's super PAC strength tips the balance, making the ratio closer to about 2 to 1.183

Priorities USA Action, a super PAC founded to help the Obama campaign, had received donations from only 12 of Obama's 532 top fundraisers as of this March. The two largest pro-Romney super PACs,

American Crossroads and Restore Our Future, have raised approximately $71 million more than Priorities.184 Priorities' lack of success can be traced to several factors within the Obama campaign. According to campaign finance specialist Anthony Corrado, many of Obama's older, more traditional donors see super PACs as encouraging negative campaign activities, and are hesitant to get involved. Obama himself has been forced at several fundraisers to explain to donors his dependence on Priorities, given his criticism of the Supreme Court's *Citizens United* decision. Republican supporters of Romney also appear to be more willing to spend any amount of money to turn Obama out of office, while Obama supporters seem to feel less passionately about preventing a Romney presidency.[185]

I expect Romney will have between $400 and $500 million to spend in what will ultimately prove to be a handful of crucial swing states. This money will allow him, of course, to run ads without disclosure and without any real review of their accuracy—as he did in the GOP primaries. The ads, in addition to damaging Obama politically, will allow Romney to insulate himself from responsibility for them.

Obama's problem is twofold. His team has done a very poor job of donor maintenance; there has been no effort to cultivate bundlers the way Clinton and both Bushes did. To some extent, this stems from his gestures at reformist politics—originally pledging not to take super PAC money, for example, and attacking independent groups, before practical realities forced him to reconsider.

But I think he and his team also share a singular disregard for the exigencies of modern-day politics: the high and mighty attitude so many have detected in Obama has surely played some role here in his inability or unwillingness to cultivate megadonors this time around. As ever, he gives off a strong impression that he should be above such tawdry considerations. Those sentiments might make him feel good, but they're not going to help him win reelection.

Where, then, does Obama look to make up his super PAC deficit? He has two main sources to look to, both of whom are now showing signs of stepping forward to make a strong funding push: major liberal donors, including George Soros; and unions.

Fortunately for Obama, after a slow start, super-wealthy liberal donors are finally showing signs of wanting to make a difference in campaign 2012. Most significantly, Soros himself, after a long period of reluctance, has reentered the fray. Soros recently announced $1 million donations to America Votes, a liberal coordinating group, and American Bridge 21st Century, the David Brock–led super PAC. These were his first donations of 2012 and are expected to portend more, both from him and other donors who may have been on the sidelines previously. Overall, such donors could provide as much as $100 million to various liberal groups during the campaign.186

What's fascinating about the recent liberal push is that—shades of 2004—the focus seems likely to be more on grassroots organizing and voter-turnout efforts than on paid advertising. For Democrats, the return of Soros and the ramping up of liberal-group efforts has to be heartening. But those with some memory of history might also be worried. Because it was this same approach in 2004—focusing much more money on grassroots organizing than on campaign ads—that may well have spelled defeat for the Democrats, when they were at the brink of victory. Democratic groups spent their money organizing up front and were caught flat-footed (and underfunded) when the GOP's Swift Boat ad campaign got underway.

"Culturally, the left doesn't do Swift Boat," said Soros advisor Michael Vachon. "It's not what we do well. If we did do it well, George W. Bush would not have been re-elected because he was a supremely swift-boat-able candidate. We don't do it well."[187]

Soros, like many other prominent liberal donors, dislikes negative ads and bemoans the changes wrought by *Citizens United*. He has always preferred the grassroots organizing focus, for example—an area where Democrats are widely seen to have an advantage over Republicans. And donors from the Democracy Alliance—a liberal group making decisions about where to steer this money—believe that, no matter how much money they raise, they will not be able to match the spending on negative ads that American Crossroads, Americans for Prosperity, and the Chamber of Commerce will do in 2012. They will stake their bets instead on grassroots, get-out-the-vote efforts.188

Interestingly, some leading Democrats—including Senate majority leader Harry Reid—are deeply worried about this approach. They believe that the liberal groups' focus on grassroots efforts will duplicate efforts the Obama administration is making along the same lines—and leave few resources to counter the expected Republican super PAC advertising onslaught.

"Why would they rule out this tried-and-true medium?" said David Krone, Reid's chief of staff, speaking of television advertising. "I can guarantee the Republicans are covering all bases and will have a coordinated plan."189

This grassroots emphasis—at the expense, ultimately, of paid advertising—is the same tactic Democrats adopted in 2004, especially down the stretch, when Republican independent expenditures buried them with negative ads. Democrats will have to hope the 2012 strategy produces a happier ending.

Obama also can count on a huge, impassioned funding push from unions, a staunch Democratic special-interest group that came out big for him in 2008. Democrats will have to rely on unions even more in 2012, making them even more beholden to this special interest. The unions have been disappointed, and sometimes infuriated, by some of Obama's policies in office; but with the fall campaign looming, they now seem ready to step forward to work for his reelection.

This deserves a closer look. As I've written at length in this book about the right-leaning super PACs and megadonors, it's only fair to examine the key role unions figure to play on the liberal side in 2012.

UNIONS: THE DEMOCRATS' ATM

Labor's enthusiasm for Democratic causes this year is remarkable when you consider that at this time last year, it looked as if a rift was forming between unions and the Democratic Party. Labor's disappointment with Obama for supporting free-trade agreements with both Colombia and South Korea is well documented. The South Korean trade deal was particularly divisive as it set some unions against one another—the AFL-CIO and the United Auto Workers, for instance, came down on different sides of that issue. Unions were also angered by Obama's failure to fight more effectively for card-check legislation, which he supported nominally but put little political capital on the line to get it passed. The bill died in the Senate.

Many union officials felt Obama neglected labor interests during his presidency. In September 2011, AFL-CIO president Richard Trumka stated that he would not be raising any money for the Democratic

National Convention. On Obama's Jobs and Competitiveness Council, labor organizers such as Trumka found themselves ignored. They felt that Obama was more focused on deficit reduction than job creation. Jeffrey Immelt, the chair of the council, came under fire for outsourcing jobs. In the fall of 2011, unemployment rates led to union anger at the president and sometimes at each other. Labor's frustrations with the stagnant economy and other setbacks overshadowed some of Obama's achievements for unions—perhaps most important, his bailout of the auto industry in Detroit, saving thousands of union jobs.[190]

Obama's efforts to play to the center have aroused union suspicions. Rose Ann DeMoro, executive director of National Nurses United, summed up the feeling of many in organized labor: "He's basically trying to be everything to everybody. . . . Until you look at the policies, and then it's clear he's there for the corporate sector."[191]

But now, with the prospect of a Mitt Romney presidency, the unions have rallied around the Democratic Party and especially President Obama. Trumka recently said that the AFL-CIO was putting together a "permanent campaign structure" that would target "real friends," "acquaintances," and "enemies." Trumka made clear that the union considered Obama a "friend."[192] Unions across the board are following suit.

Organized labor plans to involve grassroots participants like never before. Unions and their affiliated super PACs plan to spend $400 million, if not more, to help elect Democrats.[193] AFSCME alone aims to spend $100 million and mobilize at least four hundred thousand volunteers to work for the president's reelection in 2012.[194] In April, Trumka's AFL-CIO announced the launch of a new super PAC, which will use fourteen thousand different work sites around the country to mobilize both union and nonunion members. The PAC will use social media and estimates that it has raised approximately $5.4 million. The AFL-CIO expects to be able to raise more money because of looser regulations on super PACs, which will allow them to mobilize nonunion workers in addition to union workers. [195]

Why the renewed union enthusiasm for Obama and Democrats? The causes are clear: first, labor continues to prefer Democrats overwhelmingly to Republicans, and Obama has been a more pro-labor president than Bill Clinton. Second, the Republicans have made clear how much worse things could get for labor if they prevail in November.

Unions have rallied to Obama in the face of GOP initiatives in Ohio and Wisconsin to curb union collective bargaining power. The unions went from being at best tepid supporters of Obama and the Democrats to enthusiastic supporters—further tying labor to the Democratic Party. Already, unions have spent over $40 million on a successful attempt to repeal the Ohio law that limited collective bargaining rights and get a recall election approved in Wisconsin—an effort that ultimately failed to oust Governor Scott Walker.

When Walker attempted to curb union power, he became engaged in a tumultuous power struggle with union leaders. Now, facing a recall vote, Walker has become a symbol of the conflict between unions and the GOP. This struggle will likely play out on a larger scale during the general election, as union groups involved in the Walker dispute are strong supporters of Obama and those defending Walker are involved with the Romney campaign. And thanks to *Citizens United,* for the first time ever, these groups will be able to significantly affect the presidential election. Unions will pour money from their treasuries to campaign on behalf of Obama.[196]

The SEIU will be, as always, a key player. The union endorsed Obama in November 2011.[197] SEIU president Mary Kay Henry stated that the early endorsement was meant to convey to voters that they face a "stark choice" come November: "This early decision was meant to make crystal clear what kind of country we want and we think Obama is going to help make that vision a reality," she said. Because of looser restrictions this year, the SEIU will reach out to nonunion voters in an attempt to gain support for Obama. Henry failed to disclose at the time of the endorsement how much money the union will spend, saying simply: "We are trying to do it on a scale that we have never done before."[198] But the union seems poised to match or exceed its $85 million investment of 2008.

The SEIU has also teamed up with Priorities USA, the major pro-Obama super PAC, to buy airtime for anti-Romney ads in Florida and Nevada. The union is one of Priorities' biggest backers, donating $500,000 to the group in December. The close relationship between Priorities USA and the SEIU highlights the incestuous relationship between big labor and the Democratic Party; President Obama signed an executive order that encouraged using labor in large government construction projects, and he does not support right-to-work states.

As impressive as these numbers are, they may not reflect the full extent of the union financial investment in 2012. Marrick Masters, a professor at Wayne State University who studies labor and politics, believes that labor will likely spend close to *$1 billion* during 2012. "If you factor in all the personnel at the state and local level and all the costs of using those personnel, all the PAC money, all the independent expenditures . . . you are probably going to see labor spending close to $1 billion on political activity, including lobbying at the local, state and national level in 2012," he said.[199]

Clearly, then, union financial muscle will be essential to Obama's reelection drive, and to Democratic fortunes generally. With Obama's donors refusing to give to super PACs, and unions growing more powerful and politically involved, Obama probably has no choice but to rely heavily on the unions for campaign financing. Given the amount the unions seem poised to raise in 2012, it's likely that Obama, should he prevail, will owe his reelection to the support of organized labor.

●●●●●●●

THE MOST EXPENSIVE, MOST NEGATIVE ELECTION EVER

If there were no super PACs, this election would still feature campaigns spending record sums of money on vitriolic attacks. Since 1996, spending on presidential elections has grown almost exponentially. The figure more than doubled from 2002 to 2004, and then nearly doubled again from 2004 to 2008.

Campaigns have also become more negative; no election featured more negative ads—in total number—than did the 2008 election, where 68 percent of statements made in ads by the Obama campaign were negative (the second-highest percentage in history, behind Eisenhower's 1952 campaign, where 69 percent of statements made in ads were negative). John McCain too, ran a largely negative campaign, with 62 percent of statements made in his ads being negative.[200]

These numbers are not anomalies, but rather continuations of a general trend stretching back several elections. Super PACs, however, are serving as catalysts. A good encapsulation of this was the Florida GOP primary, where super PACs spent heavily. Romney's super PAC, Restore Our Future, spent $15.3 million on anti-Gingrich ads. In 2008, McCain spent a total of $11 million on ads for the entire primary cycle.201 A super PAC in one state spent more money on negative ads attacking one candidate than did an entire *winning* primary campaign four years ago. In 2008, 6 percent of the ads in the Republican primary were negative. This cycle, that number was above 50 percent.[202]

Unless and until serious action is taken, super PACs are here to stay. They will continue to shape not only single campaigns, but also whole election cycles.

It bears repeating: super PACs are not *officially* connected with any campaign. This allows them to do the dirty work without the candidate or his campaign being officially involved. Although it's obvious to even a moderately astute observer that super PACs are closely connected with candidates, the absence of official communication between super PACs and campaigns gives candidates plausible deniability. Super PACs can go negative without doing much damage to their preferred candidate's reputation—further encouraging them to go negative.

Combine the increasingly competitive and negative nature of this election cycle, and the fact that now individuals, corporations, and unions can donate unlimited amounts of money, and you have the recipe for an election so expensive that it will mark the beginning of a new campaign epoch in which courting the wealthy and special interests is paramount.

Citizens United gave our elections to the moneyed interests. Super PACs are allowing the super rich and the large special-interest groups to have an outsized influence, leveraging their wealth to effectively control our elections. Super PACs have aggravated the worst aspects of American politics. Elections are more vicious, average Americans have less of a say, and the fundraising and disclosure process is more nebulous than ever. In the upcoming election, expect to see all this play out, giving us the nastiest, costliest, most secretive election in American history.

7

The Megadonors and Their Goals

As this book was being completed, the 2012 general election season was just getting underway. In past cycles, prominent individuals have played an increasingly significant role in bankrolling candidates' campaigns, whether through 527 groups prior to 2010, or since 2010, through super PACs. The 2012 GOP primaries made abundantly clear that this model was not about to change. In fact, every sign is that the general election will be not only a furious, orgiastic spree of campaign spending but also a demonstration of the power of individual wealth in shaping U.S. elections.

What follows in this brief chapter are profiles of megadonors, the men—and so far they are all men—who have played the most prominent role in the 2012 races. It is entirely possible, of course, that others will come to the fore before the campaign is over. Only shortly before this book was finalized, George Soros, for example, announced that he would begin making major donations to liberal outside groups in an effort to ensure Democratic victories in 2012. But whatever other figures emerge before November, the individuals profiled here have made clear that they will be heard from as the campaign unfolds.

●●●●●●●

MAJOR DONORS ON THE RIGHT

Sheldon Adelson

Adelson and his wife, Miriam, have emerged as the largest donors of the 2012 presidential race: as this book was being finalized, they had given $25 million to Republican groups.203 Most of that—$23.8 million—went to Newt Gingrich's super PAC, Winning Our Future.204 With Adelson's money, Gingrich bankrolled a wave of attacks against Mitt Romney in the GOP primaries and kept himself in contention after early losses in Iowa and New Hampshire. The big infusion of Adelson cash, and a favorable electorate, propelled Gingrich to a dramatic win in South Carolina. To date, Adelson has not contributed to Romney's super PAC, Restore Our Future, and it remains to be seen how active he will be for the rest of the 2012 campaign. But he is a man of strong convictions, and so it is likely that he will play a significant role.

"The likelihood," he told *Forbes* in February, "is that I'm going to be supportive of whoever the candidate is," and he suggested that he might donate tens of millions more in the coming months.[205] That would mean giving to Romney's campaign, of course.

Who is Sheldon Adelson? He is the chairman and CEO of the Las Vegas Sands Corporation and the eighth-richest person in the United States, a self-made billionaire with a net worth of $24.9 billion, according to *Forbes*.[206] The son of Ukrainian-Jewish immigrants, Adelson got his start on Wall Street before founding Comdex, a computer trade show in Las Vegas that brought in millions as the personal-computer industry took off in the 1980s. With this initial wealth, he bought the Sands casino in 1989 and began to build a casino empire that stretches from Vegas to China and Singapore.[207] Adelson's wealth took a major hit during the Great Recession; he was overleveraged and saw his net worth fall from $28 billion to just $3 billion. But he weathered the storm and has fortified his personal wealth back to pre-recession levels.

Adelson is a relatively new player to presidential politics, first becoming active in 2007. He provided a majority of funding (nearly $30 million) for Freedom's Watch, a 527 created to counterbalance the efforts of George Soros and other Democratic donors.[208] In 2010, he gave $1 million to American Solutions for Winning the Future, a Gingrich-run PAC. He somewhat defensively told *Forbes*: "I'm against very wealthy people attempting to or influencing elections. But as long as it's doable I'm going to do it. Because I know that guys like Soros have been doing it for years, if not decades."[209]

What motivates Adelson? In his eighties, why does a man of such wealth bother spending money on American politics when, barring catastrophe (and he's already come through one in 2008), he and his businesses should thrive?

Adelson has three motivating political passions: defending the free market and countering union influence, and supporting Israel. "U.S.

domestic politics is very important to me," he has said, "because I see that the things that made this country great are now being relegated into duplicating that which is making other countries less. . . . I'm afraid of the trend where more and more people have the tendency to want to be given instead of wanting to give." He is a major contributor to the Zionist Organization of America and the Republican Jewish Coalition. Adelson, who opposes a two-state solution, was called "Benjamin Netanyahu's unofficial ambassador to the GOP" by the *New York Times*.[210] He owns an influential newspaper in Israel and contributes large amounts to Israeli charities.

As far as Israel goes, Adelson's political passions may be shaped by the issue of Iran and the ongoing conflict over its nuclear program. Adelson sees the Obama administration, which has at times had a tense relationship with Netanyahu, as hostile to the state of Israel. Meanwhile, Adelson will likely look more kindly on Mitt Romney for his longstanding ties to Prime Minister Netanyahu and his unqualified support for Israel. Depending on what occurs, if anything, between Iran and Israel before November, Adelson's role in the general election might become every bit as consequential as it was in the GOP primaries.

Harold Simmons

After the *Citizens United* ruling, when Karl Rove was working to set up American Crossroads, one of the first people he reached out to was Harold Simmons, a longtime dependable contributor to Republican causes. That remains the case, as Simmons will compete with Adelson to be the top donor of the 2012 race. According to OpenSecrets.org, Simmons and his wife had given a total of $13.7 million as of April 2012,[211] though Simmons himself claims to have contributed even more—$18.7 million as of late March.212 This includes $14.5 million to American Crossroads and roughly $1 million to each of the major Republican presidential candidates—a notable contrast to Adelson, who almost solely supported Gingrich. Simmons has freely announced that he plans to give twice as much by the end of the presidential campaign, which would bring his total contributions to $37.4 million—and make him one of the largest individual contributors to a presidential campaign in history.

Simmons is the thirty-sixth richest person in the United States, with a net worth of $9 billion, according to *Forbes*.[213] He owns Contran Corporation, a Texas-based metal and chemical conglomerate. Simmons got his start in business with a small drugstore that he turned into a chain of stores in the 1970s. He eventually sold this chain for $50 million.[214] He specializes in exploiting business opportunities that require little equity and significant debt.[215]

Simmons has been contributing to Republican candidates and causes since the 1980s, but his donations have risen dramatically over the last decade. His most significant contribution came during the 2004 race, when he gave $3 million to the Swift Vets and POWs for Truth, making him the group's second largest contributor behind Bob Perry.216 In 2008, he gave nearly $3 million to the American Issues Project, an independent group that ran ads highlighting Obama's connection to former Weatherman radical William Ayers.[217]

As his support for the Swift-Boaters shows, Simmons has no compunction about funding negative ads. (In this he differs from Adelson, who says, at least publicly, that he wants his money to go to positive ads.) Simmons has even publicly stated that he regrets that there weren't *more* negative attacks against Obama during the last election cycle.[218] If history is any guide, his money will likely power the most visceral attack ads of 2012.

Simmons's key political awakening came in 1983, when the U.S. Labor Department blocked his use of employee pension funds to acquire a sugar company, claiming the investment was too risky. Simmons decided to use his own funds to make the acquisition; the deal ultimately netted him millions of dollars that would have otherwise gone to those employees. He saw the episode as a lesson about government regulation and interference, and his political activity has followed along those lines since. The *New Republic* characterized his views as "a bland Chamber of Commerce–style business-friendly conservatism." He holds more centrist positions on social issues and describes himself as pro-choice.

Bob J. Perry

As of mid-April 2012, Perry was the third largest donor of the 2012 race, with total contributions of $6.6 million. He is the biggest financial backer of Restore Our Future, the super PAC supporting Mitt Romney, having given $3 million.[219] In 2011, he gave $2 million to American Crossroads.[220] Since 2001, he has given $2.5 million to Texas governor Rick Perry.[221]

Bob J. Perry is the owner of Perry Homes, a Texas-based homebuilder.[222] A former history teacher and football coach, Perry founded his company in the 1960s. It has since grown into the twenty-fourth largest homebuilder in the country, as of 2010, with revenues of roughly $360 million.[223] Perry is the perennial big donor in Republican politics, having given $72 million since 2000—a figure that rivals Sheldon Adelson and exceeds Harold Simmons.[224] This includes at least $28 million to local and state candidates in Texas and roughly $44 million on the national level.[225] A longtime backer of Texas governors George W. Bush and Rick Perry, Bob Perry became more active in presidential politics with the emergence of the 527s in 2004. That year, he gave $3 million to Progress for America and $4.45 million to the Swift-Boat Vets.[226] He was also an early contributor to Rove's American Crossroads, with a $7 million donation in 2010.[227]

As one might expect, Perry generally supports candidates and causes that will help create a more friendly business environment, especially as it pertains to homebuilding in Texas. He has contributed significantly to tort-reform efforts and is perhaps best known for his involvement in the Texas Residential Construction Commission. According to the *Texas Tribune*, "his corporate counsel helped craft legislation that endowed the commission with its powers, and the governor later appointed that attorney to help manage the agency. . . . Consumer groups had attacked the commission—which had been presented as a venue for protecting home owners—for lacking the power to address shoddy construction complaints."

The Koch Brothers

Noticeably absent from the current list of top 2012 Republican donors are the Koch brothers, heroes on the Republican right and notorious elsewhere for their far-reaching, often shadowy, influence. The Kochs' absence—or seeming absence—probably means that they are coordinating their spending through Americans for Prosperity, the conservative political advocacy group they founded in 2004. AFP, of which David

Koch is the chairman and, along with his brother, the founder, is officially a 501(c)(4)—a "social-welfare" organization, technically not a super PAC—that is not obligated to disclose its donor lists or the full extent of its electioneering activity. Such 501(c)s are legally restricted in terms of their involvement in campaigns, but they face limited oversight and transparency requirements, allowing organizations like AFP to skirt election laws. According to the campaign watchdog website Open Secrets:

> Like many (c)(4) groups, AFP attacks candidates through their positions on issues, rather than calling explicitly for their election or defeat. . . . Ads paid for by the AFP Foundation [AFP's associated 501(c)(3)] in 2010 added another layer of deniability by not even naming candidates but instead going after "the pork barrel stimulus" and "wasteful spending." Democrats that year complained that the Foundation's ads sometimes went up in congressional districts where ads sponsored by AFP itself (which did name candidates) had just finished running, and reinforced similar messages.228

David and Charles Koch, co-owners of Koch Industries, are jointly listed by *Forbes* as the fifth-richest people in the United States, with a net worth of $25 billion.[229] Unlike Adelson, Simmons, and Perry, the Koch brothers are not self-made; they inherited and then built upon the wealth of their father, the founder of the predecessor to Koch Industries. Under the brothers' leadership, the company expanded from an engineering firm involved mostly in oil-related work into a business conglomerate involved in a broad array of activities related to manufacturing, refining, and distribution. It was the second largest privately held company in the United States as of 2011.[230]

Both brothers hold libertarian views, emphasizing free-market solutions and individual liberty. In an acclaimed and controversial profile, Jane Mayer of *The New Yorker* called them "the primary underwriters of hard-line libertarian politics in America."[231] David Koch was also the Libertarian Party candidate for vice president in the 1980 presidential election. As libertarians, the Koch brothers deviate from traditional conservative and Republican orthodoxy in several areas: they support gay marriage, stem-cell research, and legalizing recreational drugs. They are best known, however, for their hard-core libertarian economic views. David Koch has called Obama "the most radical president we've ever had as a nation . . . and has done more damage to the free enterprise system and long-term prosperity than any president we've ever had."

Analysts on both the right and left dispute the full extent of the Kochs' political activities. They are well known as the most important backers of the Tea Party movement and for supporting various anti-union initiatives that swept the country in 2011, most notably Wisconsin governor Scott Walker's effort to limit public employees' collective bargaining rights. A PAC associated with Koch Industries was the second largest contributor to Walker's election campaign.[232] Charles Koch also helped found and fund the conservative Cato Institute and has contributed heavily to research that denies climate change. According to *The New Yorker*, the brothers have given $196 million in total to free-market advocacy organizations.[233]

The conservative *Weekly Standard* disputes some of these claims, describing the Koch brothers as a convenient scapegoat for liberals who do not understand the grassroots backlash against their policies.[234] If the Kochs' role has been overstated, this is in part their own fault, as they have gone to great lengths to conceal the extent of their political activities.

Their habit of obfuscation makes it unlikely that the full extent of their involvement in election activities in 2012 will be understood.

According to Open Secrets, AFP spent $40 million attacking Democratic candidates in 2010 and $50 million in 2011. Of the group's 2010 revenue, Open Secrets was able to determine the source of only 25 percent of its funding. There is no way to determine if the other $30 million came from the Koch brothers themselves or other sources. Koch efforts in 2012 may dwarf these previous figures. According to reporting from Politico.com: "The billionaire industrialist brothers David and Charles Koch plan to steer more than $200 million—potentially much more—to conservative groups ahead of Election Day."[235]

A good case can be made that, taking everything into account, the Koch brothers have become the most influential force in Republican politics.

Karl Rove

Karl Rove, the strategist behind George W. Bush's 2004 victory, is also the architect of the modern super PAC. After the 2008 election, Rove began to strategize about what he perceived as a lack of sufficient Republican 527 activity compared to that of the Democrats.[236] He and former Republican Party chairman Ed Gillespie quickly moved to take advantage of the *Citizens United* ruling—setting up American Crossroads, a 527, and Crossroads Grassroots Policy Strategy, a 501(c)(4) social-welfare organization. The two political operatives crossed the country in search of big donors and received an influx of funds after one private meeting in Dallas, according to the *Wall Street Journal*, in which Rove told a group of millionaires and billionaires: "All of us are responsible for the kind of country we have."[237]

While setting up American Crossroads, Rove also began to try to coordinate the efforts of several large Republican PACs through a group that became known as the Weaver Terrace Group—after the address of Rove's home in Washington, where the group held its first meeting. They now meet at the American Crossroads headquarters in downtown Washington. Initially composed of American Crossroads and four other PACs, the Weaver Terrace Group eventually expanded to thirty organizations—including the Kochs' Americans for Prosperity, the Chamber of Commerce, and American Action Network (which shares office space with American Crossroads).[238]

These groups were initially hesitant to share their strategies until American Crossroads in June of that year, at Rove's insistence, laid out its plan for various Senate races. The Chamber of Commerce then began to focus on House races, while other PACs filled in gaps as needed. In total, these groups spent $187 million in 2010, compared to the Democrats' $90 million, and are credited with helping Republicans take back the House that year.

The Weaver Terrace Group is now coordinating for the 2012 campaign. American Crossroads raised $51 million in 2011 and, along with Crossroads GPS, aims to raise between $200 million and $300 million for the election.[239] These groups will almost certainly significantly outspend their Democratic rivals. In addition to playing a major role in the presidential election, they will make it difficult for Democrats to retain the Senate and recapture the House. Karl Rove, more than any single individual, will be responsible for any Republican successes in 2012.

So far, it is not shaping up as a great landscape for Obama in terms of super-rich donors, although things have improved somewhat recently. As I documented in Chapter 6, the president will likely have to rely on major union funding support and the support of both the traditional Democratic Party campaign committees and special-interest money. The Obama-supporting super PAC, Priorities USA Action, lags far behind the Romney-backing Restore Our Future in fundraising and will almost certainly not be able to match it financially. But with the combination of unions, elite liberal donors, Democratic committees, and limited super PAC and other independent-expenditure groups, the Democrats may yet be able to make things work.

The most positive sign for Obama and the Democrats is the reentry of Soros, even if the financier's plan to focus most of his money on grassroots organizing instead of political advertising has some Democrats feeling uneasy.

George Soros

One of the world's richest men, George Soros is also one of the most controversial. A Hungarian-born child survivor of the Holocaust, he has made his billions as a financier, gaining nations' ire for shorting their currencies and other supposed market manipulations. At the same time, he has used his fortune to become a philanthropist with few rivals. His charitable organization, the Open Society Foundation, has channeled some $7 billion into a staggering array of causes—from supporting the

Polish Solidarity movement, to providing Russian universities with access to the Internet, to assisting New York artistic and educational organizations, to supporting Pakistani flood victims.

Soros has been credited and condemned for his philanthropic activities, which, according to some of his critics, seek to unravel capitalism and democracy in favor of a one-world government. But it is his bankrolling of left-wing political organizations in America that has made Soros a lightning rod for populist agitation.

Soros's deep political involvements date to 2004, when he declared that he would devote himself to defeating George W. Bush's reelection attempt. He explained in an interview with the *New York Times*: "The government of the most powerful country on earth has fallen into the hands of extremists." He proceeded to give $15.8 million to anti-Bush groups and promised to give more if necessary. Most of this money was funneled into the 527 organizations Americans Coming Together and the MoveOn.org Voter Fund, since they were some of the only means through which such large quantities of money could legally be spent on the election.[240]

Soros therefore set in motion what would become an enormous wave of 527 contributions. His clout and fame paved the way for others to join him, demonstrating the potential for 527s to receive massive contributions from incredibly wealthy donors. By the end of the 2004 elections, Soros had spent $17 million.

In 2005, he pulled back considerably, donating only half a million dollars. By 2006, however, he had ramped spending back up to $3.2 million. The 527 money went to a variety of causes, including the founding of the Secretary of State Project, which sought to elect Democratic secretaries of state in battleground states where John Kerry had lost by slim margins. The organization focused on that office because it presides over elections in each state, giving it significant influence over the outcome.241 Soros donated nearly $1 million in hard-money contributions to federal candidates and PACs, along with undisclosed donations to organizations such as Catalist LLC, the Democratic voter-database and consulting agency, and the Democratic Alliance, which shelled out millions to liberal think tanks and media groups.242 But most of his 527 money—nearly $2.2 million—went to America Votes, a progressive voter-registration and mobilization group.[243]

Soros's modus operandi of funneling his money through a variety of 527s and PACs remained the same from year to year. In 2008, Soros ramped up his spending again to assist the Obama campaign, giving at least $5 million to 527s.[244] Soros-funded groups played a number of advertisements in favor of Obama and against McCain, including a controversial ad entitled "General Petraeus or General Betray Us?" which was eventually condemned by Congress.[245]

In 2010, however, Soros announced his official exit from partisan politics. In a brief interview, he explained to the *New York Times* that he was pulling out because, fittingly, he did not think that the odds were in his favor, no matter how much money he pumped into Democratic causes. Although Soros seemed determined to move on to policy rather than electoral goals, his record of partisan contributions set a precedent and established a network that will continue to influence elections for years to come.

And now, with so much at stake in 2012, Soros has decided that he can't sit this one out. What financial support he eventually provides remains to be seen.

Jeffery Katzenberg

Although he will probably be surpassed by Soros, Katzenberg is currently the single largest Democratic donor of the 2012 election, giving $2 million to Priorities USA Action in May of 2011.[246] He has also hosted fundraisers for President Obama in his Hollywood mansion, with such guests as Steven Spielberg, Tom Hanks, and J. J. Abrams.[247]

Katzenberg is the CEO of DreamWorks Animation and a former chairman of Walt Disney Studios. He worked his way up through the movie industry in the 1970s, overseeing Disney's animation unit during what is sometimes called the "second golden age of animation" in the late 1980s and early 1990s, and finally leaving in 1994 to found DreamWorks with Steven Spielberg and David Geffen.

According to Open Secrets, Katzenberg has been an active funder of Democratic causes for two decades:

Since the 1990 cycle, Katzenberg, along with his wife Marilyn, has donated more than $2.3 million [not counting donations for the 2012 election] to federal Democratic candidates and parties and Democratic-aligned groups, according to the Center's research. That includes a $100,000 contribution during the 2004 election cycle to MoveOn.org's federally focused 527 committee. And during the 2010 election cycle alone, the Katzenbergs donated $225,100 to Democratic candidates and committees, the Center's research indicates.[248]

Impressive as that is, it's clear from those figures that Katzenberg does not have either the wealth or the desire to match the most powerful Republican fundraisers—maybe because he sees the elections in less all-or-nothing terms. Although clearly a Democrat, his primary motivation doesn't seem to be defeating Republicans for the sake of defeating them, but to blunt what he feels is an overwhelming spending advantage. Regarding his $2 million donation, he told CBS News in April: "I was concerned about the attempted hijacking of the elections by Karl Rove, the Koch brothers, and other extreme right-wing special interest money and felt strongly that a defense had to be mounted."[249] If he really wishes to do this, however, he has some ground to make up.

Priorities USA Action

Bill Burton, the former Obama deputy press secretary, and Sean Sweeney, Rahm Emanuel's chief of staff in the White House, are the two key political operatives behind the Obama-supporting super PAC Priorities USA Action. Both left the White House in February 2011 to set up their own consulting firm. Then, in April of that year, they established Priorities USA Action, a 527, and Priorities USA, a 501(c)(4), with the intention of both copying and countering Karl Rove's American Crossroads and Crossroads GPS.[250] They reached out to large funders, and they received a $2 million donation from Jeffery Katzenberg.[251] At a time when the president still openly opposed such outside-spending groups, the two defended their choice to set up a super PAC.

Our groups were formed to answer the hundreds of millions of dollars Karl Rove and the Koch brothers have dedicated to spending in the 2012 election. In 2010, Republicans spent millions distorting the debate on important issues and running vicious, dishonest attack ads. This is an effort to level the playing field and not allow right-wing activists to hijack the political system. We are simply trying to give an equal voice to the American middle-class and supporting policies that reflect America's core value of fairness.[252]

Burton has held a number of senior communications posts and was surprisingly passed over for press secretary in 2011, prompting him to leave the administration. He served as the 2008 campaign national press secretary and before that was a member of then-Senator Obama's staff.[253] Sweeney, a longtime close associate of Emanuel, has worked for Senators Schumer and Clinton and was a key player on the 2006 Democratic Congressional Campaign Committee, which retook the House that year.[254] Harold Ickes, Bill Clinton's former deputy chief of staff and a pioneer in the use of 527s during the 2004 presidential campaign, and Paul Begala, the longtime Clinton strategist, also play important roles in Priorities.[255]

Priorities USA Action and its affiliated social-welfare arm initially aimed to raise roughly $100 million, but the organizations are falling far short of that goal. As of May 2012, they had raised only $9 million. The president's own fundraising efforts have significantly outpaced his Republican rivals, making him less dependent upon the largesse of big donors and possibly explaining Priorities' lackluster performance. Nevertheless, Obama's election campaign reversed course on super PACs in February 2012 and publicly called for large donors to support Priorities.

Explaining this reversal, campaign manager Jim Messina said: "Over the last few months, super PACs affiliated with Republican presidential candidates have spent more than $40 million on television and radio, almost all of it for negative ads. . . . With so much at stake, we can't allow for two sets of rules in this election whereby the Republican nominee is the beneficiary of unlimited spending and Democrats unilaterally disarm."[256] Messina's sentiments echo those of big Republican donors, who similarly lament the state of campaign finance and frame their own efforts as a necessary response to Democratic fundraising in past election cycles.

Priorities had its best fundraising month in March, after Obama's announcement, and it may now pick up some momentum.257 Besides Katzenberg, Amy Goldman (an accomplished gardener, author, and conservationist) and Bill Maher (the comedian and HBO host) are the only million-dollar contributors to Priorities USA.[258] Maher appears to have done this at least partly for the purpose of discussing it on his TV show.

David Brock and American Bridges

David Brock, the former self-described right-wing hit man turned liberal institution builder, is the founder of American Bridges, a 527, and American Bridges 21st Century Foundation, a 501(c)(4).259 Brock made a name for himself at the conservative *American Spectator* magazine in the early 1990s. He published a book in 1993 attacking Anita Hill and then in 1994 turned his sights on the Clintons, joining what they called the vast "right-wing conspiracy." He played a role in breaking stories about Paula Jones and Troopergate. Then, in 1997, Brock did an about-face, disavowing his past work, questioning his own reporting methods, and publicly apologizing to those he might have hurt. He rebranded himself, and in 2004—with financial help from Soros—founded Media Matters for America, a watchdog group dedicated to waging an all-out campaign of "guerrilla warfare and sabotage" against conservative media outlets, particularly Fox News.[260]

Cast in the best light, Brock is a political operative and progressive seeking to atone for past transgressions by building durable liberal institutions. Viewed less generously, he is a political opportunist with few core beliefs who seeks to build counterparts to the right-wing machine he once served. His shift from right to left was at least partly pragmatic. Regarding his efforts to make amends with the Clintons, a friend of his told *New York Magazine*: "It wasn't that he wanted forgiveness from the Clintons. . . . He wanted in. He wanted to be part of this progressive restoration, and the only way he could do that was to seek reconciliation from the Big Dog and his wife."[261] Brock has apologized to those he once attacked on the left, but one wonders whether he will someday apologize to those on the right whom he may have similarly defamed in the process of building a new liberal attack machine.

Beyond serving as a counterweight to right-wing institutions and helping to reelect Obama, it is unclear what deeper purpose or beliefs guide Brock's actions. According to *New York Magazine*:

> Despite the fact that Brock has now spent a decade firmly ensconced on the left, he remains uncomfortable talking about the political issues that define it. "I have never had a serious conversation with him about policy or public philosophy," says one prominent Democrat. "I have absolutely no clue what his ideological moorings are. I don't offer it as a critique of the guy, but I just literally don't know."[262]

American Bridges has raised nearly $5.8 million for the 2012 election, less than Brock had originally planned.263 Brock has in the past proven to be an exceptional fundraiser. Media Matters counts among its funders many of the largest Democratic donors (Soros, Peter Lewis, and Stephen Bing) and brought in $23 million in donations in 2010 alone.[264] If Brock can successfully tap this donor base, American Bridges could become the most significant liberal super PAC. For now, it has been forced to scale back its efforts and is mostly focused on opposition research.[265] As this book was being finalized, Soros announced a $1 million grant to American Bridges.

For all of the power of super PACs—these shadowy organizations on which it is often difficult to put a face—it is easy to forget that the new world of campaign money is, in the end, shaped by individuals. These individuals are among the wealthiest and most powerful people in the world. They have worked on their own or in concert with party committees or party luminaries to deploy huge sums of unregulated and often unreported money with the express purpose of shaping election outcomes in the United States.

Taking into consideration their wealth, their determination to put it to political use, and the new post–*Citizens United* framework that allows them to do so in unprecedented ways, the megadonors clearly comprise a new superclass of disproportionate influence in American politics. They're part of a larger process, to be sure—one that includes national and global economic forces and a massive failure of elite political leadership—that is fundamentally disenfranchising the American electorate. The superclass and the systems it supports and manipulates have made American democracy unrepresentative and unresponsive to ordinary people. Individual voters have long pondered whether their vote really counts; they have less say now than ever.

8

Solutions and What's at Stake

It is not difficult to understand the substance of the law or the choices before Congress. Do people want to see candidates like Newt Gingrich knocked from the lead in Iowa with millions of dollars in largely negative TV ads from super PACs, which Gingrich decried until a billionaire friend gave $5 million to a pro-Newt super PAC before the upcoming South Carolina primary? Do they want to see public financing as a way that non-wealthy candidates can run for federal office? Do they want to see corporations banned from spending money on ballot measures in states like California? Do they want to see limits imposed on all political donations and expenditures to prevent corruption? Do they want to see all money—above the smallest donations—flowing in and out of campaigns and electioneering reported in a timely way?

Steven Rosenfeld, *Salon*[266]

The era of "super PACs" and secret donors has made public financing more urgent. A system that greatly magnified small donations with high matches would give ordinary citizens a shot at competing with corporations, unions and wealthy donors. It would allow candidates to campaign more instead of constantly begging among the rich. And it would give a challenger a chance to be competitive without the help of a super PAC.

New York Times, May 5, 2012

By March 2012, two months into the GOP presidential primaries but with an entire election season yet to come, Americans had already seen all that they wanted to see of super PACs. In an ABC News–*Washington Post* poll conducted just after the Super Tuesday primaries, 69 percent of Americans agreed that super PACs should be illegal—not curtailed, not reformed, but illegal.[267] More than half of the respondents (52 percent) said that they felt "strongly" about it. The results were all the more striking for their bipartisan nature: even 69 percent of self-identified Tea Party supporters, usually opponents of government regulation, wanted super PACs outlawed.

It's no wonder. Even within a population that notoriously pays little regular attention to politics—let alone primary politics—super PACs have been just about impossible to ignore. At the time the poll was conducted, super PACs were estimated to have spent $75 million on the 2012 election cycle, almost all of it—nearly $70 million—on the presidential contest. As I've discussed, super PAC spending caught up with regular candidate campaign spending and soon enough left it far behind. All of the remaining GOP presidential candidates in 2012 saw their own campaigns outspent by super PACs—in most cases, by several multiples.

In a sense, what Americans told the pollsters in March 2012 was that their original suspicions about the Supreme Court's ruling in the *Citizens United* case had been borne out. At that time—January 2010—80 percent in an ABC-Post poll said that they disagreed with the ruling. Nearly three-quarters (72 percent) said that they would support "legislative efforts to reinstate campaign spending limits the court had lifted." And the 69 percent of Americans who want to see super PACs outlawed should tell us something else, too: that reform efforts would receive widespread support from the electorate.

The question, then, is a practical one: what can be done to reform the landscape that super PACs have created? Already, a wide range of remedies have been proposed—several of which I'll explore below. A *New York Times* editorial in early May 2012 called for reviving the now-moribund public-financing system for campaigns. Pointing out that 2012 was the first presidential election since the Nixon era in which both candidates would forsake public financing, the *Times* suggested that all was not lost if general-election grants to candidates could be doubled or tripled through various matching strategies and if, similarly, primary campaign matches could be increased as well.[268] Other ideas include everything from forcing 501(c)(4) groups to disclose their donors to empowering the Justice Department to investigate (and punish) illegal coordination between political campaigns and super PACs.

At the risk of speaking too broadly, I generally support all of these ideas, at least conceptually. In essence, however, three main reform avenues are being explored: amending the Constitution, enacting legislation that forces better disclosure and other changes, and strengthening enforcement and oversight capabilities at the agency level—particularly the Federal Communications Commission.

As the dominance of super PACs over the 2012 campaign became obvious, calls for an amendment to the U.S. Constitution that would in some way rein in campaign spending became more frequent. Even the White House—trying to soft-pedal its adoption of super PAC support in the president's reelection fight—has voiced tentative support for such a step: "The President opposed the *Citizens United* decision," wrote Obama's campaign manager, Jim Messina, on the reelection website. "He understood that with the dramatic growth in opportunities to raise and spend unlimited special-interest money, we would see new strategies to hide it from public view. He continues to support a law to force full disclosure of all funding intended to influence our elections, a reform that was blocked in 2010 by a unanimous Republican filibuster in the U.S. Senate. And the President favors action—by constitutional amendment, if necessary—to place reasonable limits on all such spending."[269]

As of late January, twenty-three states had passed measures calling on Congress to "pass a constitutional amendment to reassert and elevate the political speech of individual citizens and roll back the growing legal privileges of corporations," as Steven Rosenfeld wrote in *Salon*.[270] Ten such amendments have been proposed in Congress to date. They vary widely, but they all tend to fall into one of two categories, as Rosenfeld describes: those that push back against *Citizens United* by reasserting Congress's and the states' right to regulate campaign financing, and those that more broadly seek to overturn the rights of corporate personhood by declaring "the rights protected by this Constitution to be the rights of natural persons." Doing this, of course, would then invalidate the "speech" rights that corporations enjoy now under various Supreme Court rulings, since only constitutionally recognized persons can have such speech rights.

Of the first variety, several efforts are worth noting briefly. Congresswoman Donna Edwards of Maryland and Senator Tom Udall of New Mexico, both Democrats, focus their amendment language on making clear that Congress and the states are not constitutionally prohibited from regulating campaign financing—counter to the reading the Supreme Court has given over the years. Thus Edwards's proposal begins with an explicit statement that "Nothing in this Constitution shall prohibit Congress and the States . . ." But Edwards's focus is on corporations, and it doesn't address the presence of individual billionaire benefactors like Sheldon Adelson or Foster Friess, who have become so identified with super PACs. Udall's proposal does.

At the moment, the only bipartisan effort is a House bill sponsored by Democrat John Yarmouth and Republican Walter Jones. Like the efforts of Edwards and Udall, their bill makes clear that money is not speech and authorizes Congress to enact a public financing system for political campaigns.

The second category of amendment proposals, as Rosenfeld groups them, is typified by a bill from Senator Bernie Sanders and Congressman Ted Deutch. Their amendment makes clear that corporations do not have personhood and seeks to ban all election spending by "corporate and other private entities." Interestingly, however—and perhaps ironically—their bill leaves an exception for nonprofits, the kind of entity that Citizens United was when it made the film about Hillary Clinton that launched the landmark court case. Other proposals would strip these constitutional rights from both for-profit and nonprofit corporations. As Rosenfeld points out, there is irony here, too—because if such amendments were in force in the early 1960s, they "could have stopped the NAACP from operating."

I won't go deeply into the details of these multiple proposals, but I'd support, in a broad sense, constitutional amendments that asserted Congress's right to regulate campaign financing. Without question, the wording and substance of such an amendment would have to be undertaken with the greatest care.

Many on the political right believe that no such amendment could pass constitutional muster: any restrictions on corporate speech represent, to them, a violation of First Amendment guarantees of free speech. James Taranto of the *Wall Street Journal* speaks for many when he describes the "McCain-Feingold law's unconstitutional ban on corporate political speech" and refers to the idea of getting money out of politics as "imposing governmental restrictions on political speech."[271]

In fact, Taranto took me on directly in his *Wall Street Journal* column in May 2012. Noting my criticism of the aborted Joe Ricketts–led ad campaign against Obama (which I discussed in Chapter 6), Taranto objected to my "advocacy of government censorship of political speech, the kind of expression that is at the core of First Amendment protection." I wanted to censor political speech, he wrote, based on my "disapproval of its content."[272] It's true that I found the racial content of the abandoned Ricketts ads offensive; and one of my arguments in this book is that, when political money is allowed to flow so freely, with such minimal limits and disclosure, nastier political campaigns are inevitable.

But nasty ads are a byproduct of super PACs. They are not the problem itself, but a symptom of the problem.

As this book should make clear, my opposition to super PACs is not content-based; it is process-based. It has to do with democracy.

I'm no constitutional scholar, and neither are most Americans. But it seems to me that even a rudimentary understanding of the document—and of the history of the nation's founding—ought to make clear that men like Jefferson, Madison, Adams, and Washington would never have intended the First Amendment to be read so as to guarantee multibillion-aires unrestricted access to our political system. Jefferson was forever railing against the threat of "concentration," whether of government power or financial might. Madison wrote eloquently in *The Federalist*, particularly in the famous Federalist No. 10, of the dangers of "faction"—of political special interests attaining inordinate power over the process.

What do super PACs represent but this scenario that Madison warned about?

I concur with many, both on the left and on the right, who believe that our campaign system—perhaps our constitutional system—has gone seriously off the rails because of the influence of super PACs. Free and fair elections define our democracy and are worthy of constitutional protection. The question, as always, is how to do it right.

Two other serious problems arise, too, with the constitutional route: first, as suggested above, the devil is in the details—and amending the Constitution of the United States is almost always a process rife with devils. Writing in the *New York Review of Books*, Elizabeth Drew highlights one of the most serious drawbacks of a constitutional remedy: that in attempting to change the meaning of the First Amendment, we might make things worse:

The fatal flaw in all such suggestions is the assumption that the forces of good will remain in control of any tinkering with the First Amendment . . . the idea of fixing the First Amendment in order to ban corporate funds, as several of these proposals aim to do, is altogether likely to lead to those funds being put into another form of contribution and still finding their way into the campaigns.

And it sets a very bad precedent. The Founders in Philadelphia wisely made it difficult to change this core document, by requiring the vote of two thirds of both the Senate and the House and ratification by three fourths of the states. They sought to protect the Constitution from being subject to shifts in popular opinion. Once the precedent is set, what is to keep countervailing forces from pressing for, say, a change in the First Amendment that would remove what remains of the constitutional wall between church and state?[273]

Drew's objections are shared by many others who condemn super PACs—many, if not most, on the progressive left. The problem, for them, is that a constitutional amendment is bound to cause other problems. As Harvard Law School constitutional scholar Laurence Tribe puts it, "Most of the constitutional amendments floating around seem to be seriously misguided; they would do both too much and too little." Tribe's comment is notable not only on the merits, but also as a reflection of how seriously skeptical even liberal elites are of the prospects of amending the Constitution constructively, at least in this area.

Finally, of course, even if substantive concerns can be overcome, and enough intellectual and political support can be garnered, any amendment would still have to get through the exacting process set forth under the Constitution: a two-thirds majority in both the House and Senate and then a *three-fourths* majority of the state legislatures. That's an awfully high bar, and one that tends to get cleared only by amendments a good deal less controversial than any campaign finance–related measure. There is a reason, after all, why the Constitution has only twenty-seven amendments—and ten of those are the original Bill of Rights. It's a supremely difficult battle to win, even when one has what seems like the strongest case.

Drew's misgivings aside, if a constitutional amendment managed somehow to get out of the Congress with a two-thirds majority, I'd imagine that it would steer well clear of the substantive violations she imagines. That's because in order to gain such a majority, it would have to be written extremely narrowly. If it were, I can well imagine supporting it. But alas, I seriously doubt we'll see anything like this happen.

If not an amendment, then what? There are some other, more direct routes to addressing the pervasive influence of super PACs in our politics.

●●●●●●●●●

LEGISLATIVE REMEDIES AND LOCAL ACTION

A constitutional amendment wouldn't be needed to address at least some of the problems surrounding super PACs. And given the difficulty of changing the Constitution, finding less sweeping remedies makes more sense. Several legislative efforts are underway.

In Congress, these efforts have focused on heightening the scrutiny under which super PACs operate. "We're now living in a world created by the *Citizens United* decision, and it's a disaster for our democracy," said New York Democratic senator Charles Schumer (although as a longtime beneficiary of campaign support from Goldman Sachs, he's no stranger to powerful financial donors). Schumer announced in March 2012 that Democratic senators Al Franken and Sheldon Whitehouse would help lead a seven-member task force to explore reforms.[274] The organizing principle of legislative reform is toughening disclosure requirements.

In fact, some of the most prominent reform advocates called for disclosure reforms that could still affect the way things are done in 2012.

"Congress needs to act this year to address the problems with super PACs within the boundaries available under court decisions," said Democracy 21 president Fred Wertheimer, whom the *New York Times* calls "the country's leading proponent of campaign finance reform." Wertheimer accurately points out how the current disclosure regime allows super PACs to report their donations on a relaxed schedule that discloses donor information long after presidential primaries in affected states were over—thus depriving voters of information about such funding. "Congress needs to pass legislation that provides new disclosure requirements to ensure that secret donors financing campaign expenditures are disclosed and to solve the problem of untimely disclosure by super PACs that has arisen in the 2012 presidential elections," Wertheimer says.[275]

Wertheimer believes that such legislation should require super PACs to list their top five donors in TV ads and to make official representatives of the super PACs appear in their TV ads. His organization is also pursuing legislation that would abolish the rather specious distinction between candidate-specific super PACs—like Romney's Restore Our Future or Gingrich's Winning Our Future—and the candidate's own official campaigns. In other words, if Wertheimer is successful, candidate-specific super PACs would be treated "as affiliated with the candidate's campaign and subject to the candidate's contribution limits."[276]

The way I see it, getting anything done on super PACs in 2012 would be a small miracle, given the race for political money in an election year, not to mention the extraordinary polarization in Washington on far less contentious issues. Any serious reform likely will have to wait until 2013.

Regardless of which party holds the White House then, it's a safe bet that Senate Democrats will try again to enact disclosure legislation that imposes greater transparency requirements on super PACs. Schumer has also said that he would push for a bill that toughens the standards for coordination between super PACs and campaigns. Current law bans explicit coordination, but many feel the restraints are toothless—and they are, given how many super PACs are run by candidate-friendly aides or former associates. "This level of disclosure isn't simply inadequate, it's laughable," Schumer said.

Democrats will probably try to resuscitate the DISCLOSE bill, which they came close to passing in 2010, falling one vote short in the Senate. The DISCLOSE bill would require organizations—corporations, unions, and yes, super PACs—involved in political campaigns to reveal large-donor identities in a timely manner, as well as in all political ads for which they are paying. Democratic congressman Chris Van Hollen of Maryland has reintroduced DISCLOSE in the House and picked up 117 sponsors. Unfortunately, as yet, not one is a Republican. Opposition among Republicans is based in the argument that DISCLOSE would violate free-speech rights and political participation.

Somehow, Democrats will need to find a way to gain substantive Republican support for DISCLOSE or similar efforts—especially since, in a Republican-controlled House, Van Hollen can't even bring the bill to a vote without that support. Given the polarization in our politics, the strong feelings that surround the *Citizens United* decision, and President Obama's own decision to enlist super PAC support, no legislative remedy can afford *not* to be bipartisan. At the same time, a bipartisan agreement cannot be pursued at the expense of a genuine reform that really makes a difference. If Democrats and Republicans end up agreeing on something that everyone recognizes as window dressing, they will only have strengthened the widespread cynicism of the electorate, while doing nothing to address the problem.

Important as it is, disclosure isn't the end of the battle, anyway—as the government-transparency advocacy group OpenCongress argues:

> *Of course, requiring complete, timely disclosure of corporate and union donations to super PACs is just the tip of the campaign finance-system iceberg that needs to be fixed. Congress needs to reassert their power to regulate federal campaign spending, corporate personhood should be revoked, and a robust public-financing system should be created to ensure that citizen candidates can compete with wealthy, connected incumbents. The influence of money in politics is at the core of all other political issues, and if we want to start fixing the system we need to make campaign finance reform a bigger part of our voting decisions and political activism.*[277]

Finally, it's worth noting that some states have attempted to resist the power of super PACs. The Montana Supreme Court ruled in January 2012 that the state could regulate how corporations raise and spend money in elections. What made the ruling fascinating was how the court grounded its finding within the parameters set out in *Citizens United*— because obviously a state court cannot overrule the Supreme Court. But the Montana court argued that *Citizens United* did not render all bans on corporate speech unconstitutional: "The Supreme Court held that laws that burden political speech are subject to strict scrutiny, which requires the government to prove that the law furthers a compelling state interest and is narrowly tailored to that interest." And the court, writing in defense of a 1912 state law limiting corporate campaign spending, then went on to articulate that compelling interest, focusing on Montana's long history of resisting the influence of private corporations in public elections.[278]

Unfortunately, in June 2012, the Supreme Court ruled that *Citizens United* applies equally to state laws, reversing the Montana Supreme Court's decision and determining, in the words of the *Billings Gazette,* that "the state's century-old ban on corporate spending for or against political candidates is unconstitutional." The Court's reaffirmation of *Citizens United* is another blow to campaign-finance reform proponents.

States could go explore other legislative routes, however, such as passing laws requiring corporate shareholders to approve corporate political expenditures. As Erwin Chemerinsky, dean of the University of California, Irvine School of Law, says: "These kinds of laws have been adopted for unions. It's time to do it with regard to corporations."[279]

Like the constitutional amendment efforts, legislative proposals at every level go back to a fundamental issue: reclaiming some portion of the power that localities, states, and Congress once had to regulate campaign finance. There are multiple ways of doing this, as the many efforts nationally and locally indicate.

●●●●●●●

The final venue for potential reform of super PACs is at the agency level. Most people think of the Federal Elections Commission (FEC) when they urge stronger regulation of campaign finance, but the FEC has been so ineffective for so long that it's doubtful it will play any substantive role in changing the rules of the game. There are many reasons for this, starting with the FEC's deeply partisan makeup. The commission consists of three Democrats and three Republicans, and it predictably deadlocks on one important issue after another. Given the intense opposition of the Republicans on the panel to financial regulation of campaigns, the FEC has not even been able to institute rules in line with the minimal standards set forth under *Citizens United*.[280] Five of the six current FEC commissioners are serving expired terms; President Obama has attempted just one nomination to the commission. The Senate held it up for over a year, and the candidate withdrew.

Things are so bad at the FEC, in fact, that vice chairwoman Ellen Weintraub recently told Politico that she has come to agree with the characterizations of the FEC as dysfunctional. "My personal experience," she said, "having been here for a while, is that it didn't used to be as dysfunctional as people said it was, but now it actually is, I'm sad to say." Although she and others are confident that the FEC has the legal authority to tighten disclosure rules, her efforts to do so have come to naught: "I have tried to get us to explore some issues such as disclosure in the wake of *Citizens United*, and have been completely unsuccessful. I tried hard; I tried repeatedly, but people have strongly held views over here."[281]

Given its track record and its institutional paralysis, calls for the FEC to step in and do something before Election Day 2012 seem more than a little fanciful. Only someone willfully ignorant of how the FEC works would expect the commission to step up to the plate in this climate. But another federal agency could be brought to bear on the problem.

That agency is the Federal Communications Commission (FCC), regulator of the nation's television and radio airwaves. As the 2012 campaign has become an unmitigated fiasco for campaign finance transparency, and as the FEC's passivity shows no sign of changing, the FCC has proposed a new requirement: that broadcasters post online the name of anyone buying time for political advertising, along with the air date and amount of the purchase. It's a remarkably straightforward, simple suggestion, and it would make a real difference. Better yet, it's not even a new law, fundamentally—at most, it's an extension of current law, which requires broadcasters to make available such information when asked. The new FCC requirement would make the broadcasters' responsibilities in this area, at least as regards political advertising, more explicit and proactive.

Once the information is posted, the FCC proposes, it would store it in an agency-administered, publicly accessible centralized database. As *Bloomberg News* wrote in an enthusiastic editorial summarizing the proposal: "This would allow anyone who's interested to see who is paying for political ads, what they are paying for them and where they are being broadcast. It would also allow broadcasters to meet the public-interest obligation they bear in return for their use of public spectrum, which yielded them an estimated $2.3 billion in political ad spending alone in the 2010 campaign and will probably produce even more political revenue this year."[282]

As *Bloomberg* notes, the proposal has already met with some fairly predictable opposition. The sole Republican on the FCC's three-person commission somewhat oddly called it a "jobs destroyer." And one broadcasting group—being either disingenuous or simply ignorant of the urgency of timely disclosure—argued that anyone wishing to review a station's political-ad spending information is welcome to come down to the station in person and review it. A more relevant objection is broadcasters' concerns about publicly disclosing their pricing schedules—information commercial advertisers would appreciate having in their negotiations for ad time. But these don't strike me as remotely compelling enough reasons to resist such a sensible requirement, given the impact political money is having on campaigns. Besides, the FCC's current proposal is only for broadcast TV ads. For the time being, cable stations and radio outlets would have a free pass. But if the plan worked well, it could be extended to those channels in the next cycle.

Without question, the fact that the United States has a Federal Elections Commission that is essentially useless—so useless that other commissions are trying to pick up the slack—reflects poorly on our political system. But let's keep things in perspective: someday, maybe, we can get around to reforming the FEC. For now, let's focus on reforming campaign finance.

WHAT'S AT STAKE

For years now, pundits and commentators have lamented what they see as the disengagement and cynicism of American voters, who are so turned off by politics that they view both parties with contempt or disengage from the process. Others, as I've written in recent books, double down on partisanship and extreme ideological attachments, in the hope of reforming a system that no longer serves individual citizens. My take has been, and remains, that Americans are *right* to be cynical and disgusted—what they see is reality, not some distorted reflection of their dissatisfactions.

Money in politics—exemplified now by super PACs—is perhaps the number one reason why Americans feel the way they do. Yet for all of their disgust, when asked—as in the poll I opened this chapter discussing—they still express a clear point of view and a desire to see things change. That so many Americans of varying political viewpoints feel almost exactly the same about super PACs not only reflects the corrosive influence of super PACs; it also should show us what a rare opportunity might exist to get some genuine bipartisan reform. If Democrats and Republicans can find a commonsense, middle ground on reforms, whether legislatively or otherwise, they would almost certainly have a substantial majority of Americans on their side.

I'm encouraged by the fact that efforts are taking place on so many fronts: we need as multifaceted an approach as possible, with the goal of maximizing disclosure.

Generally speaking, as I indicated earlier, my position here is less about arguing the deep details of the various proposals, but to indicate my broad support for efforts in the main reform areas being discussed: constitutional amendment, legislative remedies, and agency reforms. What shape these efforts take now is up to those whom we elect.

But if there is anything I'd like the reader to take away from this book, it is this: if we don't do something to change the current arrangement, we are going to lose American democracy as we all have known it. Already, in my view, that democracy is deeply compromised, wounded, and much less effective and responsive than ever before. We are also losing our core values about one-person, one-vote and about elections as broad referenda on the direction of the country and reflections of the people's endorsement of one direction or another for the future. It's hard to believe in these things when, increasingly, the candidates put before us are funded so heavily by people like Sheldon Adelson, Harold Simmons, and the Koch brothers, or by George Soros, a few other liberal benefactors, and left-wing labor unions.

It's getting tougher to run for office, tougher to get on the ballot, tougher to debate the real issues. With the advent of super PACs, it's simply tougher to have fair elections. As the Annenberg study that I cited earlier pointed out, negative advertising—the overwhelming majority of it from Mitt Romney–supporting super PACs—dominated the Republican primaries and for all practical purposes, determined the outcome. Restore Our Future's role in the GOP primaries is merely the latest instance of outside groups essentially hijacking our elections: in 2004 we had the Swift-Boat group; in 2006 and 2008 the unions made an overwhelming push, and in 2008 we also saw a shattering of all campaign finance records for Obama's presidential campaign; in 2010, groups like American Crossroads and the Club for Growth wielded outsized influence.

Now we face a critical presidential election, at a time when the country struggles with enormous, historic problems, and every indication is that outside groups—both left and right—will again shape the outcome. These groups all have their special pet issues, whether it's free-market, anti-regulatory policies for big business or favorable union legislation; regardless of what their goals are, they see no disconnect between the pursuit of their own narrow interests and the pursuit of the national interest. It is simply tougher, if not impossible, to address the genuine issues that matter to millions of Americans in a system controlled and managed by elites—especially when the political messaging is so heavily dominated by outside groups.

The voice of the ordinary American voter is scarcely heard over the din of super PAC messaging. We have a less democratic and less responsive system.

This is truly a tragedy: unless something is done soon, and substantively, our political system will complete a catastrophic descent from democratic republic to American casino.

Postscript: June 2012

As this book is finalized, it appears almost certain that Republican super PACs will raise somewhere between $250 billion and $500 billion for campaign 2012, if not more.

Meanwhile, the Obama campaign seems to have realized, perhaps belatedly, that it will be outspent substantially in the general election. Since the Romney campaign can concentrate the bulk of its spending in the ten to twelve swing states most in play, its disproportionate super PAC spending advantage will be felt to an even greater degree.

Pro-Republican independent expenditures also played a key role in the June 2012 Wisconsin recall election, where they helped expand the size of Governor Scott Walker's victory. And while his triumph cannot be attributed solely to money, the financial disparity between the two parties clearly made a big difference. The recent Supreme Court decision limiting the union checkoff of political expenditures will also make it more difficult for Democrat-affiliated unions to raise and spend the resources necessary to compete effectively.

All of this suggests that the political environment that characterized the Republican primaries—super PAC money having a disproportionate, if not dispositive, influence—could prevail again in November 2012.

Notes

INTRODUCTION: THE END OF AMERICAN DEMOCRACY?

1   *Citizens United v. Federal Election Commission*, 558 U.S.
2   http://abcnews.go.com/Politics/abc-news-poll-romney-pulls-obama-head-head/story?id=13776546&page=2.
3   http://www.whitehouse.gov/photos-and-video/video/limiting-influence-special-interests#transcript.
4   http://www.boston.com/2012/02/07/obama/TXeV6IqiVlPH8ELnJ68KyK/story.html.
5   Potter is quoted from an interview on National Public Radio, February 23, 2012, http://www.npr.org/2012/02/23/147294509/examining-the-superpac-with-colberts-trevor-potter.
6   http://www.huffingtonpost.com/2011/09/26/super-pacs-secret-money-campaign-finance_n_977699.html.?view=print&comm_ref=false.
7   http://www.usatoday.com/news/washington/2010-06-25-finance_N.htm.
8   http://www.campaignlegalcenter.org/index.php?option=com_content&view=article&id=1469:september-26-2011-huffington-post-super-pacs-and-secret-money-the-unregulated-shadow-campaign&catid=64:press-articles-of-interest&Itemid=62.

CHAPTER 1: HOW SUPER PACS CHANGED EVERYTHING

9   http://www.opensecrets.org/pacs/lookup2.php?strID=C00384701.
10   http://www.politico.com/news/stories/0911/64448.html.
11   http://sapper.blogspot.com/2012/02/roll-over-joseph-goebbels-make-way-for.html
12   http://www.opensecrets.org/news/2011/05/citizens-united-decision-profoundly-affects-political-landscape.html.
13   According to OpenSecrets.com, nonprofit, tax-exempt groups organized under section 501(c) of the Internal Revenue Code can engage in varying amounts of political activity, depending on the type of group. For example, 501(c)(3) groups operate for religious, charitable, scientific, or educational purposes. These groups are not supposed to engage in any political activities, though some voter registration activities are permitted. 501(c)(4) groups are commonly called "social-welfare" organizations that may engage in political activities as long as these activities do not become their primary purpose. Similar restrictions apply to Section 501(c)(5) labor and agricultural groups, and to Section 501(c)(6) business leagues, chambers of commerce, real estate boards and boards of trade.
14   http://www.huffingtonpost.com/the-center-for-public-integrity/crossroads-groups-raise-w_b_1245575.html.
15   Comment made while being interviewed by Chris Matthews on MSNBC's *Hardball*, February 27, 2012.
16   http://www.nytimes.com/2012/02/02/us/politics/super-pac-filings-show-power-and-secrecy.html.?_r=1&pagewanted=2.

17   "Secrecy Shrouds 'Super PAC' Funds in Latest Filings," *New York Times*, February 1, 2012, http://www.nytimes.com/2012/02/02/us/politics/super-pac-filings-show-power-and-secrecy.html.?pagewanted=all.

18   "What Super PAC Filings Left Out," Politico.com, February 3, 2012, http://www.politico.com/news/stories/0212/72420.html.

19   "Super PAC Disclosures Are Too Little, Too Late," United Republic, February 1, 2012, http://unitedrepublic.org/2012/super-pac-disclosures-are-too-little-too-late/.

20   "Attack Dog," *The New Yorker*, February 13, 2012, http://www.newyorker.com/reporting/2012/02/13/120213fa_fact_mayer?currentPage=all.

21   Astute political watchers will also recall that Dukakis was photographed wearing an ill-fitting helmet in the turret of a tank with a geeky smile. This was also used by the Bush campaign to buttress his weak credentials on defense.

22   "Attack Dog," *The New Yorker*, February 13, 2012.

23   "The Reinvention of Political Morality," *New York Times,* December 5, 2011. http://campaignstops.blogs.nytimes.com/2011/12/05/the-reinvention-of-political-morality/.

24   http://www.politifact.com/truth-o-meter/statements/2011/nov/22/mitt-romney/mitt-romney-says-obama-said-if-we-keep-talking-abo/.

CHAPTER 2: SWIFT-BOATING THE SYSTEM: THE 2004 ELECTIONS

25   http://projects.iwatchnews.org/index.htm/projects.publicintegrity.org/docs/527/pdf1.pdf.

26   http://online.wsj.com/article/SB119802611610438187.html.

27   http://www.cfinst.org/books_reports/EAR/pdf/EAR_527Chapter.pdf.

28   Ibid.

29   Janofsky, M., "Advocacy Groups Spent Record Amount on 2004 Election," *New York Times,* December 17, 2004.

30   Ibid.

31   Stephen Weissman and Michael Malbin, *BCRA and the 527 Groups*, Campaign Finance Institute, February 9, 2005

32   Ibid.

33   Ibid.

34   Ibid.

35   Ibid.

36   S. R. Garret, E. Lunder, and L. P. Whitaker, *Section 527 Political Organizations*, Congressional Research Service, February 8, 2008.

37   Weissman and Malbin, *BCRA and the 527 Groups*.

38   Not counting the Joint Victory Campaign 2004, which served as the fundraising arm of the other two.

39   "America Coming Together, 2004 Election Cycle," Open Secrets, http://www.opensecrets.org/527s/527events.php?id=10.

40   "The Media Fund, 2004 Election Cycle," Open Secrets, http://www.opensecrets.org/527s/527events.php?id=15.

41   "MoveOn.org, 2004 Election Cycle," Open Secrets, http://www.opensecrets.org/527s/527events.php?id=41.

42   http://www.usatoday.com/news/politicselections/nation/president/2004-09-07-texas-ad_x.htm.

43   Weissman and Malbin, *BCRA and the 527 Groups*.

44	M. Janofsky, "Advocacy Groups Spent Record Amount on 2004 Election," *New York Times,* December 17, 2004. A. Knott, A. Pilhofer, and D. Willis, "GOP 527s Outspend Dems in Late Ad Blitz," Center for Public Integrity, November 3, 2004, http://www.iwatchnews.org/2004/11/03/5544/gop-527s-outspend-dems-late-ad-blitz.
45	Weissman and Malbin, *BCRA and the 527 Groups.*
46	"Swift Vets & POWs for Truth: Top Contributors, 2004 Cycle," Open Secrets, http://www.opensecrets.org/527s/527cmtedetail_contribs.php?ein=201041228&cycle=2004.
47	Ibid.
48	Weissman and Malbin, *BCRA and the 527 Groups.*
49	D. Yadron, "Bob Perry Gives $7 Million to American Crossroads," *Wall Street Journal,* October 20, 2010, http://blogs.wsj.com/washwire/2010/10/20/bob-perry-gives-7-million-to-american-crossroads/.
50	Weissman and Malbin, *BCRA and the 527 Groups.*
51	Garret, Lunder, and Whitaker, *Section 527 Political Organizations.*
52	Weissman and Malbin, *BCRA and the 527 Groups.*
53	"Progress for America, 2004 Election Cycle," Open Secrets,http://www.opensecrets.org/527s/527events.php?id=6.
54	Knott, Pilhofer, and Willis, "GOP 527s Outspend Dems in Late Ad Blitz."
55	J. Keen and M. Memmot, "Most Expensive TV Campaign Ad Goes for Emotions," *USA Today,* October 18, 2004, http://www.usatoday.com/news/politicselections/nation/president/2004-10-18-adwatch-ashley_x.htm.
56	"Swift Boat Veterans for Truth, 2004 Election Cycle," Open Secrets, http://www.opensecrets.org/527s/527events.php?id=61.
57	http://web.archive.org/web/20041012040319/http://www.swiftvets.com/script.html.
58	http://left.wikia.com/wiki/America_Coming_Together.
59	N. Gibbs et al., "In Victory's Glow," *Time,* November 15, 2004.
60	G. Korte, "Now That It's Over, We Can Laugh," *Cincinnati Enquirer,* November 7, 2004.
61	A. C. Smith, "Party People: 20 Hours of Sketches and Observations from Election Day 2004," *St. Petersburg Times,* November 7, 2004; Ted Byrd, "Candidates Lay Groundwork," *Tampa Tribune,* June 20, 2004.
62	It does not include America Coming Together (ACT), the largest 527 of 2004, which was primarily focused on Democratic get-out-the-vote efforts.
63	http://select.nytimes.com/gst/abstract.html.?res=F40913F63D5D0C7A8EDDAB0994DC404482.

CHAPTER 3: DEMOCRATIC MUSCLE: OUTSIDE MONEY IN 2006 AND 2008

64	http://online.wsj.com/article/SB124243785248026055.html.
65	Both Democratic and Republican 527s roughly split their expenditures between federal races—meaning House and Senate—and state races such as gubernatorial and state legislative elections.
66	http://www.cfinst.org/books_reports/pdf/NP_SoftMoney_0608.pdf.
67	http://www.seiu.org/a/ourunion/fast-facts.php.
68	http://www.factcheck.org/2010/08/service-employees-international-union-seiu/.
69	http://www.motherjones.com/mojo/2008/02/seiu-picks-obama.
70	http://www.historylearningsite.co.uk/527-elections.htm.
71	http://www.opensecrets.org/pacs/lookup2.php?strID=C00004036&cycle=2006.
72	http://www.opensecrets.org/pacs/indexpend.php?cmte=C00004036&cycle=2006&txt.

73   http://www.nytimes.com/cq/2007/03/09/cq_2388.html.?pagewanted=all.
74   http://www.opensecrets.org/races/indexp.php?cycle=2006&id=MTS1.
75   http://www.opensecrets.org/outsidespending/recips
       php?cmte=C00011114&cycle=2006.
76   http://www.cfinst.org/books_reports/pdf/NP_SoftMoney_0608.pdf.
77   http://www.billyelenak.com/rjwrite/040906move.html.
78   http://rothenbergpoliticalreport.com/news/article/moveon.org-pressuring-democrats-
       in-health-care-fight.
79   http://www.opensecrets.org/pacs/lookup2.php?strID=C00401224.
80   "Heavy Hitters: Act Blue," Open Secrets, http://www.opensecrets.org/orgs/summary.
       php?id=D000021806.
81   http://www.cfinst.org/press/PReleases/06-11-01/Federal_527s_raise_131_million_32_
       more_than_in_2002_election.aspx.
82   Ibid.
83   Ibid.
84   http://www.cfinst.org/books_reports/pdf/NP_SoftMoney_0608.pdf.
85   http://www.cfinst.org/pr/pdf/527/527-12G_Table3.pdf.
86   Ibid.
87   http://articles.cnn.com/2008-06-19/politics/obama.public.financing_1_public-financ-
       ing-obama-campaign?_s=PM:POLITICS.
88   http://www.cfinst.org/Press/PReleases/08-11-24/Realty_Check_-_Obama_Small_
       Donors.aspx.
89   http://www.beachwoodreporter.com/politics/obamas_small_donor_myth.php 90
       http://www.cfinst.org/press/preleases/09-02-25/Soft_Money_Political_Spending_by_
       Nonprofits_Tripled_in_2008.aspx.
91   http://online.wsj.com/article/SB124243785248026055.html.
92   http://www.opensecrets.org/outsidespending/recips.
       php?cmte=C00004036&cycle=2008.
93   http://www.opensecrets.org/orgs/toprecips.php?id=D000000077.
94   http://online.wsj.com/article/SB124243785248026055.html.
95   Ibid.
96   Ibid.
97   http://www.npr.org/templates/archives/archive.php?thingId=127308724.
98   http://www.cfinst.org/press/preleases/09-02-25/Soft_Money_Political_Spending_by_
       Nonprofits_Tripled_in_2008.aspx.
99   Ibid.
100   http://articles.latimes.com/2008/nov/02/nation/na-chamber2.
101   http://www.bloomberg.com/apps/news?pid=newsarchive&sid=aIxU19LXZBa4&refer=us.
102   http://www.theatlantic.com/politics/archive/2009/10
       /exclusive-how-democrats-won-the-data-war-in-2008/27647/.
103   http://online.wsj.com/article/SB124243785248026055.html.

CHAPTER 4: THE *FIRST CITIZENS UNITED* ELECTION: 2010

104   http://www.leahy.senate.gov/press/press_releases/release/?id=5c07ee6a-ef6f-4e41-
       b1c5-e95cfbbb386c.
105   http://www.huffingtonpost.com/2012/03/27/john-mccain-citizens-united-campaign-
       finance_n_1383230.html.?ref=elections-2012.

106 http://thecaucus.blogs.nytimes.com/2010/10/26/union-spends-91-million-on-midterms/.
107 http://www.washingtonpost.com/wp-dyn/content/article/2010/12/03/AR2010120306995.html.?hpid=topnews.
108 http://www.opensecrets.org/pacs/superpacs.php?cycle=2010.
109 "Mission," American Crossroads, http://americancrossroads.org/mission.
110 "Outside Spending. American Crossroads," Open Secrets, http://www.opensecrets.org/outsidespending/detail.php?cmte=American+Crossroads%2FCrossroads+GPS&cycle=2010.
111 Michael Beckel, "Karl Rove–Linked Conservative Group, American Crossroads, Adapts to New Campaign Finance Landscape," Open Secrets Blog, August 19, 2010, http://www.opensecrets.org/news/2010/08/karl-rove-linked-conservative-group.html.
112 http://64.e5bed1.client.atlantech.net/527s/527cmtedetail_contribs.php?cycle=2010&ein=050532524.
113 Beckel, "Karl Rove–Linked Conservative Group, American Crossroads."
114 http://www.factcheck.org/2010/08/american-crossroads/.
115 Justin Elliott, " 'Grassroots' Rove–Linked Group Funded Almost Entirely by Billionaires," Salon, http://www.salon.com/2010/07/23/rove_group_billionaire_donors/.
116 http://blogs.wsj.com/washwire/2010/10/20/bob-perry-gives-7-million-to-american-crossroads/.
117 http://blogs.newsobserver.com/wakeed/national-democratic-super-pac-donated-money-in-wake-county-school-board-runoff.
118 "Pro-Growth Tax Policy," Club for Growth, http://www.clubforgrowth.org/philosophy/.
119 Ibid.
120 "Club for Growth Summary," Open Secrets, http://www.opensecrets.org/pacs/lookup2.php?strID=C00432260.
121 http://www.politicsdaily.com/2010/05/11/bob-bennett-club-for-growth-utah-power-player/.
122 http://factcheckutah.wordpress.com/2011/07/28/op-ed-senator-mike-lee-and-our-club-for-growth-future/.
123 http://www.opensecrets.org/news/2010/10/american-crossroads-spends-big.html.
124 http://www.opensecrets.org/news/2010/11/led-by-karl-rove-linked-groups-nonp.html.
125 Ibid.
126 http://www.opensecrets.org/outsidespending/recips.php?cmte=Club+for+Growth&cycle=2010.
127 http://www.politico.com/news/stories/0510/37966.html.
128 http://www.denverpost.com/ci_15737667.
129 http://www.theatlantic.com/politics/archive/2010/09/what-tea-party-express-did-for-christine-odonnell/62984/.
130 http://www.opensecrets.org/news/2010/11/led-by-karl-rove-linked-groups-nonp.html.
131 http://www.msnbc.msn.com/id/39995283/ns/politics-decision_2010/#.T38vKb9Wp8g.
132 http://www.washingtonpost.com/wp-dyn/content/article/2010/10/13/AR2010101303451.html.
133 http://politicalticker.blogs.cnn.com/2010/10/13/american-crossroads-boasts-13-million-haul-for-week-starts-spending-on-house-races/.
134 http://msnbcmedia.msn.com/i/msnbc/sections/news/GOPScorecard.pdf.
135 http://www.politico.com/news/stories/1010/43545.html.
136 http://www.opensecrets.org/outsidespending/recips.php?cycle=2010&cmte=C00487744.
137 Paul Blumenthal, "Karl Rove-Linked Super PAC American Crossroads Reports July and August Donations," *Huffington Post*, http://www.huffingtonpost.com/2011/09/02/

karl-rove-kenneth-griffin-super-pac_n_946108.html.?ref=mostpopular.

138   http://www.opensecrets.org/outsidespending/summ.
php?cycle=2010&disp=O&type=U.

139   http://www.npr.org/templates/story/story.php?storyId=131039717.

140   http://www.opensecrets.org/pacs/superpacs.php.

CHAPTER 5: SUPER PACS AND THE 2012 GOP PRIMARIES

141   http://www.forbes.com/forbes/2012/0312/feature-chinese-gambling-sheldon-adelson-
billion-dollar-bet_print.html.

142   http://www.cbsnews.com/8301-503544_162-57350769-503544/gingrich-romney-
wants-to-buy-election/.

143   http://www.cnn.com/video/?/video/us/2012/03/13/tsr-erin-alabama-mississippi-ad-
spending.cnn.

144   At the end of January, ROF had $16 million on hand, compared to a paltry $7.7 million by the Romney campaign. Gingrich's Super PAC had $2.4 million in the bank,
while his campaign had $1.8 million. The Romney campaign raised $6.5 million
(Super PAC raised $12.5 million) in January, while Gingrich raised $5.5 million (Super
PAC raised $11 million).

145   http://www.newyorker.com/reporting/2008/06/30/080630fa_fact_
bruck?currentPage=all.

146   http://www.washingtonpost.com/wp-srv/special/politics/track-presidential-campaign-
ads-2012/.

147   http://www.huffingtonpost.com/2012/04/30/super-pac-attack-ads-restore-our-
future_n_1464447.html.?utm_source=Alert-blogger&utm_medium=email&utm_
campaign=Email%2BNotifications.

148   http://www.annenbergpublicpolicycenter.org/NewsDetails.aspx?myId=484.

149   http://articles.boston.com/2012-01-02/news/30581995_1_negative-ads-mitt-romney-
radio-ad.

150   http://www.cbsnews.com/8301-503544_162-57350769-503544/gingrich-romney-
wants-to-buy-election/.

151   http://www.politico.com/news/stories/0711/60329.html.#ixzz1pD1UD55l.

152   http://www.publicpolicypolling.com/main/2011/12/paul-pulling-closer-to-gingrich-
in-iowa.html.#more.

153   http://www.minnpost.com/eric-black-ink/2012/01/superpacs-outspending-candi-
dates-2-1-south-carolina.

154   http://www.washingtonpost.com/blogs/fact-checker/post/four-pinocchios-for-king-
of-bain/2012/01/12/gIQADX8WuP_blog.html.

155   http://thehill.com/homenews/campaign/227347-obama-attack-ad-steals-gingrich-
play-puts-focus-on-bain.

156   http://www.newyorker.com/online/blogs/comment/2012/01/romney-king-of-bain.
html.#ixzz1pHvmX7t9.

157   http://www.thedailybeast.com/articles/2012/01/31/romney-ramps-up-attack-ads-
against-gingrich-to-unprecedented-levels.html.

158   http://reporting.sunlightfoundation.com/super-pacs/committee/restore-our-future-
inc/C00490045/.

159   http://elections.nytimes.com/2012/campaign-finance/independent-expenditures/
week/2012-02-20.

160   http://news.yahoo.com/blogs/ticket/santorum-ad-features-romney-lookalike-gun-wielding-rombo-150340157.html.

161   http://online.wsj.com/article/SB10001424052970204653604577251272804570082.html.

162   Santorum's campaign did outspend his Super PAC in Oklahoma, Tennessee, and Georgia.

163   http://online.wsj.com/article/SB10001424052970203961204577267822228233682.html.

164   http://www.washingtonpost.com/national/alabama-mississippi-primaries-are-dominated-by-super-pac-ads/2012/03/13/gIQANXls9R_print.html.

165   http://www.politico.com/blogs/burns-haberman/2012/03/santorum-outgunned-to-in-illinois-to-in-chicago-117953.html.

166   http://www.politico.com/news/stories/0312/74430.html.#ixzz1q9J31jaw.

167   "HuffPost FundRaise—Santorum Swamped by Super PAC in Illinois," Huffington Post, http://www.huffingtonpost.com/2012/03/19/huffpost-fundrace---sant_n_1365652.html.?utm_source=Alert-blogger&utm_medium=email&utm_campaign=Email%2BNotifications.

CHAPTER 6: WHY 2012 WILL BE THE NASTIEST, COSTLIEST RACE IN HISTORY

168   http://nation.foxnews.com/david-axelrod/2012/05/08/civil-axelrod-calls-rove-contract-killer.

169   http://online.wsj.com/article/SB10001424052702303448404577407752437654514.html.

170   http://news.medill.northwestern.edu/chicago/news.aspx?id=184924.

171   http://thecaucus.blogs.nytimes.com/2012/04/16/800-million-target-for-romney-campaign-and-republican-committee/.

172   http://www.reuters.com/article/2012/04/20/us-usa-campaign-money-idUSBRE83I1ID20120420.

173   http://www.theblaze.com/stories/unions-prepared-to-spend-over-400m-to-re-elect-president/.

174   http://online.wsj.com/article/SB10001424052702303448404577407752437654514.html.

175   Ibid.

176   http://www.nytimes.com/2012/05/18/us/politics/magnate-steps-into-2012-fray-on-wild-pitch.html.

177   http://www.chicagotribune.com/topic/wgntv-la-super-pac-preparing-ads-tying-obama-to-south-side-pastor-20120517,0,1682499.story.

178   http://www.chicagotribune.com/news/local/breaking/chi-super-pac-preparing-ads-tying-obama-to-south-side-pastor-20120517,0,5880797.story.

179   http://www.politico.com/blogs/burns-haberman/2012/05/axelrod-says-ad-buy-is-million-slams-rove-and-kochs-122651.html.

180   http://www.nytimes.com/2012/04/24/us/politics/conservative-groups-spend-heavily-in-senate-races.html.

181   http://www.opensecrets.org/news/2011/05/citizens-united-decision-profoundly-affects-political-landscape.html.

182   http://www.commentarymagazine.com/2012/04/27/obama-super-pac-problems-campaign-finance/.

183   http://www.bloomberg.com/news/print/2012-04-27/clinton-backers-wait-for-obamas-to-cut-checks-for-super-pac.html.

184   http://www.bloomberg.com/news/print/2012-04-27/clinton-backers-wait-for-obama-s-to-cut-checks-for-super-pac.html.

185   Ibid.

186   http://www.nytimes.com/2012/05/08/us/politics/liberals-putting-super-pac-money-into-grass-roots.html.?_r=1&hp.

187   "HuffPost FundRace—Santorum Swamped by Super PAC in Illinois."

188   Ibid.

189   http://www.nytimes.com/2012/05/09/us/politics/liberal-donors-plan-worries-top-democrats.html.?hp.

190   http://www.thedailybeast.com/articles/2011/09/07/obama-faces-labor-union-ire-as-he-gears-up-for-2012-reelection-campaign.html.

191   Peter Wallsten, "Obama and Unions: Many in Labor Movement Frustrated with President," *Washington Post,* http://www.washingtonpost.com/wp-dyn/content/article/2011/02/18/AR2011021807480.html.

192   http://www.nationaljournal.com/2012-presidential-campaign/trumka-afl-cio-estab-lishing-permanent-campaign-structure--20120506.

193   http://www.dailykos.com/story/2012/02/22/1067282/-Unions-plan-to-spend-more-than-400-million-on-2012-elections.

194   http://articles.chicagotribune.com/2012-04-17/news/sns-rt-us-usa-campaign-labor-bre83g1h6-20120417_1_union-spending-labor-discontent-american-crossroads.

195   http://www.rollcall.com/news/labor_union_flexes_muscle_with_super_pac-213738-1.html.

196   http://www.nytimes.com/2012/04/29/us/wisconsin-vote-is-first-shot-in-wider-union-war.html.?_r=1&ref=scottkwalker.

197   http://www.seiu.org/2011/11/endorsement-2012.php.

198   http://blogs.wsj.com/washwire/2011/11/16/seiu-gives-obama-early-endorsement/.

199   http://articles.chicagotribune.com/2012-04-17/news/sns-rt-us-usa-campaign-labor-bre83g1h6-20120417_1_union-spending-labor-discontent-american-crossroads.

200   http://www.politifact.com/florida/statements/2012/feb/06/marco-rubio/marco-rubio-no-candidate-has-run-more-negative-ads/.

201   http://www.policymic.com/articles/3789/florida-primary-results-mitt-romney-wins-big-newt-gingrich-stumbles-rick-santorum-and-ron-paul-fail-to-have-impact.

202   http://www.washingtonpost.com/politics/study-negative-campaign-ads-much-more-frequent-vicious-than-in-primaries-past/2012/02/14/gIQAR7ifPR_story.html.

CHAPTER 7: THE MEGADONORS AND THEIR GOALS

203   "2012 Top Donors to Outside Spending Groups," Open Secrets, http://www.opensecrets.org/outsidespending/summ.php?cycle=2012&disp=D&type=V.

204   "Donors to Winning Our Future, 2012," Open Secrets, http://www.opensecrets.org/outsidespending/contrib.php?cmte=C00507525&type=A&cycle=2012.

205   Steven Bertoni, "Billionaire Sheldon Adelson Says He Might Give $100M to Newt Gingrich or Other Republican," *Forbes Magazine,* February 21, 2012, http://www.forbes.com/sites/stevenbertoni/2012/02/21/billionaire-sheldon-adelson-says-he-might-give-100m-to-newt-gingrich-or-other-republican/.

206   "Sheldon Adelson Profile," *Forbes Magazine,* http://www.forbes.com/profile/sheldon-adelson/.

207   Steven Bertoni, "Comeback Billionaire: How Adelson Dominates Chinese Gambling

and U.S. Politics," *Forbes Magazine*, February 22, 2012, http://www.forbes.com/sites/stevenbertoni/2012/02/22/comeback-billionaire-how-sheldon-adelson-dominates-chinese-gambling-and-u-s-politics/.

208   Michael Luo, "Great Expectations of Conservative Group Seem All but Dashed," *New York Times*, April 12, 2008, http://www.nytimes.com/2008/04/12/us/politics/12freedom.html.

209   Andrew Rosenthal, "Sheldon Adelson for Campaign Finance Reform," *New York Times*, February 21, 2012, http://loyalopposition.blogs.nytimes.com/2012/02/21/sheldon-adelson-for-campaign-finance-reform/.

210   Frank Rich, "Sugar Daddies," *New York Times Magazine*, http://nymag.com/news/frank-rich/conservative-donors-2012-4/.

211   "2012 Top Donors to Outside Spending Groups," Open Secrets, http://www.opensecrets.org/outsidespending/summ.php?cycle=2012&disp=D&type=V.

212   Charles Romans, "The Operator," *New Republic*, http://www.tnr.com/article/politics/magazine/102778/harold-simmons-campaign-donor-2012-gop.

213   "Harold Simmons Profile," *Forbes Magazine*, http://www.forbes.com/profile/harold-simmons/.

214   Charles Romans, "The Operator," *New Republic*, http://www.tnr.com/article/politics/magazine/102778/harold-simmons-campaign-donor-2012-gop.

215   Bill Bancroft, "Perils of the Simmons Watch," *New York Times*, December 1989.

216   "Swift Vets & POWs for Truth: Top Contributors, 2004 Cycle," Open Secrets, http://www.opensecrets.org/527s/527cmtedetail_contribs.php?ein=201041228&cycle=2004.

217   http://query.nytimes.com/gst/fullpage.html.?res=9C07E4DB1739F930A1575BC0A96E9C8B63&ref=haroldcsimmons.

218   Rich, "Sugar Daddies."

219   "Donors to Restore Our Future, 2012," Open Secrets, http://www.opensecrets.org/outsidespending/contrib.php?cmte=C00490045&type=A; "2012 Top Donors to Outside Spending Groups," Open Secrets, April 2012, http://www.opensecrets.org/outsidespending/summ.php?disp=D.

220   "Donors to American Crossroads, 2012," Open Secrets, http://www.opensecrets.org/outsidespending/contrib.php?cmte=C00487363&type=A&cycle=2012.

221   Massimo Calabresi, "Friends with Benefits, Rick Perry's Biggest Donors," *Time*, September 2011, http://swampland.time.com/2011/09/15/rick-perrys-friends-with-benefits/.

222   Ibid.

223   "Perry Homes, Builder Online," http://www.builderonline.com/builder100/2010/perry-homes.aspx.

224   Rich, "Sugar Daddies."

225   Matt Stiles, "Prolific Donor Has Given $66 Million Since 2000," *Texas Tribune*, http://www.texastribune.org/texas-politics/campaign-finance/prolific-donor-has-given-66-million-since-2000/.

226   "Progress for American: Top Contributors, 2004 Cycle," Open Secrets, http://www.opensecrets.org/527s/527cmtedetail_contribs.php?ein=201170395&cycle=2004; "Swift Vets and POWs for Truth: Top Contributors, 2004 Cycle," Open Secrets, http://www.opensecrets.org/527s/527cmtedetail_contribs.php?ein=201041228&cycle=2004.

227   Stiles, "Prolific Donor Has Given $66 Million Since 2000."

228   Vivica Novak and Robert Maguire, "Koch Connected Groups Show Holes in Disclosure Requirements," http://www.opensecrets.org/news/2012/03/energy-industry-trade-groups.html.

229   "Charles Koch Profile," *Forbes Magazine,* http://www.forbes.com/profile/charles-koch/.

230   "Koch Industries Profile," *Forbes Magazine,* http://www.forbes.com/lists/2005/21/VMZQ.html.

231   Jane Mayer, "Cover Operations," *The New Yorker,* August 30, 2010, http://www.newyorker.com/reporting/2010/08/30/100830fa_fact_mayer.

232   Andy Kroll, "Wisconsin Governor Scott Walker: Funded by the Koch Bros.," *Mother Jones,* February 2011, http://motherjones.com/mojo/2011/02/wisconsin-scott-walker-koch-brothers.

233   Mayer, "Cover Operations."

234   Matthew Continetti, "The Paranoid Style in Liberal Politics," *Weekly Standard,* http://www.weeklystandard.com/articles/paranoid-style-liberal-politics_555525.html.?nopager=1.

235   Kenneth Vogel, "Rove vs. The Koch Brothers," Politico, October 2011, http://dyn.politico.com/printstory.cfm?uuid=571964E7-AE37-425F-97C5-C2127CB1E566.

236   Jeanne Cummings, "Republican Groups Coordinated Financial Firepower," Politico, November 2010, http://www.politico.com/news/stories/1110/44651.html.

237   Monica Langley, "Texas Billionaire Doles Out Election's Biggest Checks," *Wall Street Journal,* http://online.wsj.com/article/SB10001424052702303812904577291450562940874.html.

238   Mike Allen and Kenneth Vogel, "Rove, GOP Plot Vast Network to Reclaim Power," Politico, May 2010, http://dyn.politico.com/printstory.cfm?uuid=6B062BE2-18FE-70B2-A8B3681BB340CE93; Jeanne Cummings, "Republican Groups Coordinated Financial Firepower," Politico, November 2010.

239   Jim Rutenberg and Jeff Zeleny, " 'Super PAC' Eying General Election, Aims Blitz at Obama," **New York Times,** April 9, 2012, http://www.nytimes.com/2012/04/09/us/politics/major-republican-super-pac-prepares-to-take-on-obama.html.?pagewanted=all; Peter Stone, "Haley Barbour Is Cranking Up His Crossroads Fundraising While Winding Down Governorship," iWatch News, November 2010, http://www.iwatchnews.org/2011/11/08/7333/haley-barbour-cranking-his-crossroads-fundraising-while-winding-down-governorship.

240   Leslie Wayne, "And for His Next Feat, a Billionaire Sets Sights on Bush," *New York Times,* May 31,2004

241   "Secretary of State Project," DiscoverTheNetworks, http://www.discoverthenetworks.org/printgroupProfile.asp?grpid=7487.

242   Kara Ryan, and Stephen Weissman, "Soft Money in the 2006 Election and the Outlook for 2008," *The Campaign Finance Institute.*

243   "George Soros Contributions to 527 Organizations, 2006 Election Cycle," Open Secrets, http://www.opensecrets.org/527s/527indivsdetail.php?id=U0000000364&cycle=2006.

244   "George Soros Contributions to 527 Organizations, 2008 Election Cycle," Open Secrets. http://209.190.229.99/527s/527indivsdetail.php?id=U0000000364&cycle=2008.

245   Perry Bacon Jr., "MoveOn Unmoved by Furor over Ad Targeting Petraeus," *Washington Post,* http://www.washingtonpost.com/wp-dyn/content/article/2007/09/20/AR2007092001005.html.?nav=hcmodule.

246   "Priorities USA Action Contributors," Open Secrets, http://www.opensecrets.org/pacs/pacgave2.php?cmte=C00495861&cycle=2012.

247   Tina Daunt, "Jeffrey Katzenberg Sets Spring Hollywood Fundraiser for President Obama," *Hollywood Reporter,* February 2012, http://www.hollywoodreporter.com/news/obama-fundraiser-jeffrey-katzenberg-dreamworks-286702.

248   Michael Beckel, "Deep-Pocketed Democratic Donors Among the First Supporters of Liberal Super PAC, Nonprofit Operation," Open Secrets, May 2011, http://www.opensecrets.org/news/2011/05/deep-pocketed-democratic-donors.html.

249   Wyatt Andrews and Phil Hirschkorn, "Jeffrey Katzenberg Explains Super PAC Donation," CBS News, April 2012, http://www.cbsnews.com/8301-503544_162-57410615-503544/jeffrey-katzenberg-explains-super-pac-donation/.

250   "Bill Burton, Senior Strategist, Priorities USA," *Washington Post,* http://www.washingtonpost.com/politics/bill-burton/gIQAFW7ZAP_topic.html.; "Sean Sweeney, Senior Strategist, Priorities USA," *Washington Post,* http://www.washingtonpost.com/politics/sean-sweeney/gIQAAqj99O_topic.html.

251   Peter Nicholas and Carol Lee, "Super PAC Money Stalled Despite Obama Green Light," *Wall Street Journal,* April 2012, http://online.wsj.com/article/SB10001424052702304750404577319570424661572.html.

252   http://www.politico.com/blogs/bensmith/0411/In_memo_Priorities_USA_defends_secretmoney_shift.html.

253   "Bill Burton, Senior Strategist, Priorities USA," *Washington Post.*

254   "Sean Sweeney, Senior Strategist, Priorities USA," *Washington Post.*

255   Aaron Mehta, "PAC Profile: Priorities USA Action," iWatch News, January 2012, http://www.iwatchnews.org/node/8025/.

256   Jeff Mason, "In Shift, Obama Campaign to Support Super PAC Fundraiser," Reuters, February 7, 2012, http://www.reuters.com/article/2012/02/07/us-usa-campaign-obama-superpac-idUSTRE81617U20120207.

257   Paul Blumenthal, "Obama-Endorsed Super PAC Priorities USA Action Improves Fundraising," April 2012, *Huffington Post,* http://www.huffingtonpost.com/2012/04/20/obama-super-pac-priorities-usa-action-_n_1442179.html.

258   "Priorities USA Action Contributors," Open Secrets, April 2012, http://www.opensecrets.org/pacs/pacgave2.php?cmte=C00495861&cycle=2012.

259   Alexandra Druszak, "PAC Profile: American Bridges 21st Century," iWatch News, February 2012, http://www.iwatchnews.org/node/8177/.

260   Jason Zengerie, "If I Take Down Fox, Is All Forgiven?" *New York Magazine,* May 2011, http://nymag.com/news/media/david-brock-media-matters-2011-5/index4.html.

261   Ibid.

262   Ibid.

263   "American Bridges 21st Century Summary," Open Secrets, May 2012, http://www.opensecrets.org/pacs/lookup2.php?cycle=2012&strID=C00492140.

264   Michael Luo, "Effort for Liberal Balance to G.O.P. Groups Begins," *New York Times,* November 23, 2010, http://www.nytimes.com/2010/11/23/us/politics/23money.html.

265   Zengerie, "If I Take Down Fox."

CHAPTER 8: SOLUTIONS AND WHAT'S AT STAKE

266   http://www.salon.com/2012/01/21/the_hard_truth_of_citizens_united/.

267   http://www.langerresearch.com/uploads/1135a3SuperPACs.pdf.

268   http://www.nytimes.com/2012/05/06/opinion/sunday/an-idea-worth-saving.
        html.?partner=rssnyt&emc=rss.
269   http://www.barackobama.com/news/entry/we-will-not-play-by-two-sets-of-rules/.
270   http://www.salon.com/2012/01/21/the_hard_truth_of_citizens_united/.
271   http://online.wsj.com/article/SB10001424052702303661904576456080297702652.html.
272   http://online.wsj.com/article/SB10001424052702303610504577418271290920422.
        html.?mod=djemBestOfTheWeb_h.
273   http://www.nybooks.com/articles/archives/2012/feb/23/can-we-have-democratic-
        election/?pagination=false.
274   http://www.rollcall.com/news/senate_democrats_criticize_super_pacs-212043-1.
        html.?zkMobileView=true.
275   http://www.huffingtonpost.com/fred-wertheimer/super-pac-disclosure-
        reports_b_1246978.html.
276   Though Wertheimer supports breaking down the distinction between candidate super
        PACs and candidate campaigns, he does not support simply undoing the limits on
        candidate contributions, which some advocate as a solution that would make super
        PACs superfluous: "It is important to recognize that the Super PAC problem cannot be
        solved by repealing the limits on contributions to candidates. Taking that destructive
        step would return us to historic campaign finance scandals of the past and a system of
        pure legalized corruption where donors could provide huge contributions directly to
        officeholders and candidates in exchange for their votes."
277   http://www.opencongress.org/articles/view/2479-Dems-Re-Intro-Super-PAC-
        Disclosure-Bill.
278   http://www.alternet.org/module/printversion/153623.
279   http://www.salon.com/2012/01/21/the_hard_truth_of_citizens_united/.
280   http://www.bloomberg.com/news/2012-02-08/as-super-pacs-rule-obama-ducks-fight-
        over-their-future-view.html.
281   http://dyn.politico.com/printstory.cfm?uuid=B7530F94-10E4-4052-8A04-
        19C5C56E4BC3.
282   http://www.bloomberg.com/news/print/2012-03-19/get-tv-political-ad-data-out-of-
        the-cabinet-onto-the-web-view.html.

Dear Reader:

Thank you for devoting some of your valuable free time to *American Casino*—I hope you found the book thought provoking.

I wrote it because I have come to believe that the power of money in our politics has become so pervasive that the future of our democratic system is genuinely threatened. Unless significant action is taken at various levels—whether constitutional, legislative, or regulatory—I fear that American democracy, at least as we have known it, will cease to exist.

Do you agree? Do you disagree? What is your response to the arguments I've laid out here?

Are you also concerned about the pervasiveness of super PACs and billionaire donors, or do you believe that attempts to regulate political giving by these entities invariably constitute censorship of political speech? Or do you have an entirely different take?

I'd love to hear your thoughts on *American Casino*, or on my other recent book, which deals with some of the same issues: *Hopelessly Divided*.

Send your comments on these or other subjects to info@ schoenconsulting.com. And to see more books, articles, and current commentary of interest, be sure to visit my Web site at http:// douglasschoen.com.

Best wishes,

Doug Schoen

More Praise for Douglas E. Schoen's Books

Hopelessly Divided: The New Crisis in American Politics and What It Means for 2012 and Beyond

"Doug Schoen is one of our most insightful analysts, and Hopelessly Divided analyzes the divisions in American politics and offers a step forward. I may not always agree with Schoen's conclusions, but I've always known him to be honest and a straight shooter. This is one of those books that is definitely worth reading to understand the 2012 election."

–Sean Hannity, *The Sean Hannity Show*

"Hopelessly Divided could well become the definitive work explaining why America has become so polarized, and it offers a real-world assessment of what we need to do to fix our politics. Doug Schoen combines the unique mix of high-level practical experience and sophisticated analytical tools to address the central question facing our dysfunctional political system."

–Joe Trippi, author of *The Revolution Will Not Be Televised*

The Political Fix: Changing the Game of American Democracy, from the Grassroots to the White House

"Very few people understand the workings of the American political system as well as Doug Schoen. For more than twenty-five years Doug has been an instrumental inside player and observer of the political scene. This book comprehensively and articulately lays out Doug's prescriptions for taking back a broken and oftentimes counterproductive system. I urge every political figure and junkie to read this important book."

–--Senator Bob Kerrey, former Nebraska governor and president,
the New School for Social Research *Declaring Independence:
The Beginning of the End of the Two-Party System*

"*The two-party system in America is breaking down, and Doug Schoen's new book, Declaring Independence, explains why. This is an in-depth look at why the American people are so fed up with partisanship, and where we, as a nation, go from here.*"

—Mayor --Michael R. Bloomberg, mayor of New York City

"*It's Independents' Day in America, and Doug Schoen works the numbers in this persuasive book to prove that anxious moderates can do more than swing elections. They are poised to smash the two- party systemand give us an independent president as early as this year.*"

—--Jonathan Alter, senior editor, Newsweek, and author of The Defining Moment